CW00322527

Response to the Reports of the Foot and Mouth Disease Inquiries

By HM Government with the Welsh Assembly Government

Presented to Parliament
by the Secretary of State for Environment, Food and Rural Affairs
by Command of Her Majesty
November 2002

Laid before the National Assembly for Wales
by the Deputy First Minister and
Minister for Rural Development and Wales Abroad
November 2002

Cm 5637   Gratis

© **Crown Copyright 2002**

FOREWORD

It is an indication of the Government's wish to learn and apply the lessons of the recent Foot-and-Mouth Disease (FMD) outbreak that, barely three months after the reports of Dr Anderson's Lessons Learned Inquiry and the Royal Society's scientific review of Infectious diseases in livestock, I am able to introduce the Government response to those reports.

It is not much more than a year since the last case of FMD. The speed with which we have been able to take stock and draw lessons from this appalling outbreak is a tribute to the hard work of the two inquiry teams. I am very grateful to Dr Anderson and Sir Brian Follett and their teams for this. We have also benefited from the National Audit Office's report, which is being considered by the Public Accounts Committee.

The Royal Society had a wide remit to review infectious diseases of livestock. Its unique contribution has given a clear and authoritative scientific basis on which to take forward the work described in this response, given from an independent standpoint.

Dr Anderson has also given us his independent view of the epidemic, and of the lessons learned. His independence is demonstrated by his sometimes trenchant comments in the report. As I made clear in my statement to the House of Commons on the report, we accept that mistakes were made. While not necessarily agreeing with every observation and comment in the two reports, we accept that there are clear lessons to be learned: for example, the need for greater flexibility in contingency planning and closer involvement of stakeholders in those plans; the need for speed in scaling up operations; better communications; and handling the vast scale of operations that were required in some areas. I also accept that we need to continue to work on cultural change in Defra.

We are determined, as this response shows, to set out programmes of work which will need to be taken forward, so that the lessons are not only learned, but also applied. Defra will do this in an open way, consulting where possible all those with an interest, to build a new framework in which outbreaks of animal diseases can be handled in partnership with the farming industry, the wider rural community and other key stakeholders such as local authorities. We accept the need for regular reviews of and reports on animal disease preparedness and will consider the mechanism for this with stakeholders.

I share Dr Anderson's hope that not only the Government but everyone with an interest in the future of farming and the wider rural economy will look to learn the lessons of the epidemic, apply the recommendations and thereby collectively ensure that the experience of 2001 is never repeated.

Margaret Beckett

Rt Hon Margaret Beckett MP
Secretary of State for Environment, Food and Rural Affairs

EXECUTIVE SUMMARY

1.   This is the Government's response, with the Welsh Assembly Government, to the reports of the Lessons Learned Inquiry into the 2001 epidemic of FMD chaired by Dr Iain Anderson and the Royal Society's Inquiry into infectious diseases in livestock chaired by Professor Sir Brian Follett.

2.   *Section 1, the Introduction and background*, puts the response in the context of two forthcoming major strategy documents. The Strategy for Sustainable Farming and Food, to be published shortly, will establish a new settlement with the farming and food industries, giving a clear direction towards a more sustainable future, and incorporating a response to each of the recommendations of the Policy Commission on the Future of Farming and Food. As called for by the Policy Commission and the two FMD inquiries, a new Animal Health and Welfare Strategy for Great Britain will provide an overall strategic approach to animal health and welfare work, with the aim of reducing the economic, social and environmental impact of animal diseases, and improving the welfare of animals kept by man. The Strategy will draw on the inquiry reports, and on discussions with a wide range of interested parties. When published in Spring 2003, it will provide an update on progress on much of the work described in this response.

3.   The Government accepts that there were mistakes in its handling of the 2001 FMD outbreak, and is determined to learn from these. It accepts virtually all the detailed recommendations of the Lessons Learned report, and firmly endorses the lessons which Dr Anderson draws. The recommendations made by the Royal Society will also play a major role in shaping the Government's work in this area.

4.   Defra is a new department, whose mission to promote the interests of rural areas will ensure that the consequences of animal disease control for the country as a whole are fully considered. It has embarked on a programme of reform to address the issues identified in the inquiry reports, and has action in hand under each of the 3 key areas identified by Dr Anderson: to ensure that <u>systems</u> are in place to handle any epidemic, with <u>speed</u> and on the basis of good <u>science</u>.

5.   The State Veterinary Service will in future work more closely with the rest of Defra and outside stakeholders to deliver its specialised and professional services.

6.   *Section 2 describes a stronger framework for emergency preparedness.* Both inquiries emphasised the need for comprehensive and co-ordinated contingency planning, with published plans that are regularly rehearsed with all concerned. The Lessons Learned Inquiry advocated an animal health legislative framework which was robust, unambiguous and fit for purpose, with a possible wider review of animal health legislation. Any such animal health framework would need to be compatible with EU policy on exotic animal diseases. It also suggested there was a fear of risk-taking within Defra and that a reappraisal of attitudes and behaviours within the Department would be beneficial. The Royal Society recommended increased spending on animal health research, and better co-ordination of research. Both inquiries called for a body to provide scientific advice to the Defra Chief Scientific Adviser in emergencies. Key points in the Government's response are:

●   The Government has established the Civil Contingencies Secretariat to co-ordinate the UK's contingency planning and help strengthen the UK's resilience at every level to disruptive challenges. The Secretariat is improving its contacts with local authorities and the Government will enhance the capacity of Government Offices from 2003 with dedicated contingency planning teams in each region.

●   Defra is publishing a revised Contingency Plan for FMD and will publish plans for other diseases. They will be available to all who may be involved in an outbreak. Defra will train staff and rehearse the plans to check they work and that all concerned can understand and use them. The

Government will lay the FMD Plan before Parliament. The Welsh Assembly Government has developed its own contingency plan. Defra will work closely with others who have a role to play, in particular local authorities with their unrivalled local knowledge.

- Defra's Risk Management Strategy sets out how the Department will deal with risk and uncertainty. Defra has worked closely with the Prime Minister's Strategy Unit in its Risk and Uncertainty project.

- The Animal Health Bill will strengthen the Government's ability to deal with any future outbreaks. The Government will address the scope and nature of future legislation next year after publication of the Animal Health and Welfare Strategy.

- The Government plans to increase spending on animal health research to underpin the development and application of policies and will consider its research priorities as part of the Animal Health and Welfare Strategy.

- An interdepartmental group will promote better co-ordination of research in the light of the current review of Defra's science based agencies and the recent review of the Institute for Animal Health at Pirbright.

- The Government will allocate £25 million over the next five years as additional funding for veterinary teaching and research.

- Defra has established a Science Advisory Group which will set up rapid and robust arrangements for advice to the Defra Chief Scientific Adviser in emergencies.

7. *Section 3 deals with strengthening disease prevention.* The inquiries called for enhancement to disease surveillance at the EU level. They also recommended action to tackle illegal meat imports and enhanced systems of control. They recommended as wide as possible an involvement of those with a role in surveillance. On animal movements, both inquiries recommended that the Government should base restrictions on wider considerations including a cost-benefit analysis. They called for a comprehensive livestock tracing system. The inquiry reports stress the importance of good biosecurity, both in terms of effective biosecurity measures and the active involvement of all those dealing with livestock. Key points in the Government's response are:

- The Government will support international efforts to improve data collection and reporting on animal diseases.

- The Government has made good progress on the illegal imports Action Plan published in March 2002 and is spending over £3 million on this in the current financial year. It launched a publicity campaign on illegal imports in July and a six-month detector dog pilot started in September.

- Defra will publish a Risk Assessment on the introduction of FMD in illegal imports later in the Autumn.

- The Government has secured tighter EU controls on personal imports of animal products.

- Following a Cabinet Office study, all activity against smuggling of meat, animal products, fish and plant matter will be brought together in HM Customs and Excise and backed by a new dedicated target in Customs for service delivery in this area. There will be substantially improved co-ordination between the main control agencies, and between these agencies and Customs, under the oversight of a new ministerial group.

- The Government recognises the strong case for a single agency to oversee all aspects of the management of legal trade. But that is not an immediate proposition, and it will seek a step change in the co-ordination and delivery of local authority inspection of imported foodstuffs and products of animal origin at ports within one year. Thereafter it will then look hard again at the case for bringing these functions from local authorities into a central agency, or delivering them from other routes.

- Defra will re-examine the Action Plan later this year in the light of the organisational changes and the results of the Risk Assessment.

- A Veterinary Surveillance Strategy is being developed. Defra is also working to identify the best use of practising vets in surveillance and developing a Geographical Information Strategy.

- The Government has commissioned a wide-ranging study to inform a decision on the role of animal movement standstills in the future.

- A new Livestock Identification Programme is being developed with the aim of improving the identification and tracing of UK livestock by introducing a single platform of animal information with electronic identification of individual cattle, sheep and, if necessary, pigs.

- Defra will develop an all-encompassing biosecurity code.

8. *Section 4 sets out the Government's plans for the emergency response and disease control in an animal disease outbreak.* The inquiries have recommended that the Government should deal with future outbreaks of FMD by culling of infected premises and dangerous contacts, but that the option of emergency vaccination should be considered as a major tool if and when this initial "stamping out" policy proves insufficient. Both reports acknowledge that there are still some obstacles to overcome before the Government could pursue an emergency vaccinate-to-live policy and recommend that the Government should address these in advance of an outbreak. Both the inquiries favour an immediate national ban on livestock movements once the first case is confirmed.

9.   The Lessons Learned Inquiry has recommended that the Government should not use mass pyres again as a strategy for disposal of slaughtered animals. The Lessons Learned Inquiry recommended that Defra should develop further its interim Contingency Plan with procedures in place to scale up communications and resources rapidly. Defra should develop its human resources plans for use in an emergency and consult the Armed Forces as soon as possible. It should have a regional communications strategy and dedicated management information systems.

10.   The Royal Society concluded that the Government should explore a range of possible disease control strategies and, so far as practicable, take decisions in advance of outbreaks as to the optimum strategy in particular circumstances. The Lessons Learned Inquiry recommended that the joint Defra Industry Working Group for Animal Disease Insurance ensure that its scope is set widely enough to address valuation and compensation issues highlighted by the 2001 outbreak.

11.   A key point in the Government's response is that the policy which it has adopted in the event of an outbreak now means that:

- Defra will alert the Armed Forces immediately a case of FMD is confirmed so that the scope of their possible involvement can be assessed.

- A national movement ban will be put in place as soon as a case of FMD is confirmed.

- The Government will apply tight biosecurity requirements in a 10km zone around infected premises by declaring Restricted Infected Areas (so-called "Blue Boxes") from the start of an outbreak.

- Public rights of way will be only be restricted within Infected Areas. The Government will issue a protocol for consultation shortly.

- The Government will dispose of culled animals by commercial incineration, rendering and licensed landfill.

12. In addition:

- The control of FMD will require the slaughter of diseased animals and other susceptible animals on the premises and of dangerous contacts - this is the 'stamping out' in EU legislation and recommended by the inquiries.

- Beyond that the Government needs a range of strategies in its armoury for different disease situations – including preventative culling powers as provided for in the Animal Health Bill and a strategy of emergency vaccinate-to-live.

- For a vaccinate-to-live strategy to work, a number of logistical, technical and trade problems need to be resolved and the Government is committed to resolving them – the Contingency Plan will cover a vaccinate-to-live strategy and the Government will develop an exit strategy for use after emergency vaccination.

13. Other key points are:

- Defra has established an Emergency Preparedness Programme to oversee a wide range of work on contingency planning.

- The Cabinet Office is developing a protocol for managing the increase of staff numbers in emergencies and is reviewing the training and development available to senior managers across Whitehall for dealing with emergencies.

- To replace current interim arrangements, Defra will develop a permanent emergency register listing competencies and skills for staff willing to serve in an emergency and will put in place appropriate management structures to allow rapid commitment of extra resources.

- Defra will communicate more clearly and effectively in a crisis.

- The Government will review and rationalise animal disease compensation arrangements. It will put forward policy options for sharing the costs of animal disease outbreaks with the industry.

14. *Annex I* sets out the Government's response to each of the detailed recommendations of the Lessons Learned Inquiry as well as the Key Findings and recommendations of the Royal Society.

15. *Annex II* describes the funding of research into animal health diseases.

16. *Annex III* covers operational aspects of emergency vaccination.

SECTION 1: INTRODUCTION AND BACKGROUND

1.1   The 2001 outbreak of FMD was a very painful experience for the nation and particularly for those in the countryside. Defra and the Government as a whole are determined to learn the lessons from that experience.

1.2   This response to the reports of the FMD inquiries shows how that learning and change is well under way. It will continue over the months and years to come.

1.3   This response contains a wide range of actions, commitments and decisions. So soon after the publication of such thorough reports, there are inevitably some areas where the Government can only report on work in progress and directions for future work.

A new approach – Strategies for Sustainable Farming and Food and Animal Health and Welfare

1.4   The response can be read on its own. But it also needs to be seen in the context of two forthcoming major strategy documents:

- The Government's Strategy for Sustainable Farming and Food in England. This builds on the report of the Policy Commission on the Future of Farming and Food, chaired by Sir Don Curry, which was itself commissioned partly in response to FMD. The Government will publish it shortly.

- A comprehensive Animal Health and Welfare Strategy for Great Britain, discussed below, which the Government expects to publish in Spring 2003.

1.5   The Policy Commission on the Future of Farming and Food and the two FMD inquiries have all called for a more strategic approach to animal health and welfare, in the light of the apparent increase in animal disease outbreaks, and the major impacts these diseases, and their control measures, have on the rest of society. The Government endorses this need, and is now engaged in developing, in consultation with the Devolved Administrations and a wide range of stakeholders, an Animal Health and Welfare Strategy for Great Britain, intended to reduce the economic, social and environmental impact of animal diseases, and improve the welfare of animals kept by man.

1.6   This Strategy will draw heavily on the analysis and recommendations of the two FMD inquiries, and link closely with the Strategy for Sustainable Farming and Food. It will bring together the strands of current and planned activity on animal disease, health and welfare, seeking more sustainable outcomes, greater partnership with stakeholders and customers, a firmer scientific and evidence base, and a better partnership and balance between public and private provision. When published next Spring the Strategy will provide an opportunity to report further progress on a number of strands of work discussed in this response.

Lessons Learned

1.7   The Secretary of State, the Rt Hon Margaret Beckett MP, has already made it clear, in her statement to the House of Commons on publication of the Lessons Learned report on 22 July, that the Government accepts that there were mistakes in its handling of the crisis, and is determined to learn from these mistakes. This response confirms her expectation then that the Government would be able to accept virtually all the detailed recommendations of the Lessons Learned report.

1.8   The Lessons Learned Inquiry summarises the major lessons from FMD 2001 as follows:

- *Maintain vigilance through international, national and local surveillance and reconnaissance.*

- *Be prepared with comprehensive contingency plans, building mutual trust and confidence through training and practice.*

- *React with speed and certainty to an emergency or escalating crisis by applying well-rehearsed crisis management procedures.*

- *Explain policies, plans and practices by communicating with all interested parties comprehensively, clearly and consistently in a transparent way.*

- *Respect local knowledge and delegate decisions wherever possible, without losing sight of the national strategy.*

- *Apply risk assessment and cost benefit analysis within an appropriate economic model.*

- *Use data and information management systems that conform to recognised good practice in support of intelligence gathering and decision making.*

- *Have a legislative framework that gives Government the powers needed to respond effectively to the emerging needs of a crisis.*

- *Base policy decisions on best available science and ensure that the processes for providing scientific advice are widely understood and trusted.*

1.9   The report says that these lessons should be incorporated into a national strategy designed to:

- *Keep out infectious agents of exotic disease.*

- *Reduce livestock vulnerability by reforms in industry practice.*

- *Minimise the impact of any outbreak.*

1.10   The Government firmly endorses these conclusions. Detailed responses to the report's recommendations are in Annex I.

Scientific aspects – the Royal Society

1.11   The Royal Society's report on Infectious diseases in livestock, published on 16 July, provides a core text on the science and control of FMD and other exotic diseases, which will prove invaluable to the scientific, Government and farming communities both here, throughout Europe and internationally. The report covers the scientific issues relating to the transmission, prevention and control of epidemic disease in livestock, covering FMD and a range of other diseases. Although science-led, the report also offers practical guidance. This is a benefit of the wide basis of the membership of the Inquiry Committee, which included those involved in farming, veterinary practice and consumer affairs as well as science.

1.12   Defra is committed to ensuring that it develops evidence-based policies which use the best available scientific information. This requires a nationally agreed research programme which underpins the needs identified in the Animal Health and Welfare Strategy. All funders will be able to refer to the Royal Society's report to guide not only their own research strategies, but also how these programmes can best be coordinated and delivered, including involvement at EU level. More widely, the Royal Society's Key Findings and recommendations will inform the Government's approach to work on animal health.

1.13   Detailed responses to the Royal Society's Key Findings and recommendations are in Annex I.

Animal Health and Welfare Strategy

1.14   The Policy Commission on the Future of Farming and Food, the FMD inquiries and external stakeholders have all called for a more integrated, coherent and strategic approach to the Government's work on animal health and disease control.

1.15   Defra's strategy on sustainable development, "Foundations for our Future", endorsed this need, and committed the Government to a strategy which set out "actions to improve the health of farmed animals through the reduction and eradication of disease, better risk management strategies, greater involvement of stakeholders in our work, and improved veterinary surveillance." The Government and stakeholders agree that it needs to cover not only disease control, but also the positive promotion of animal health and welfare.

1.16   There is much on which to build. The FMD outbreak, and the various inquiries, reviews and conferences to which it gave rise, have deepened the Government's understanding of the threats and costs of exotic diseases, the difficulties of dealing with them, the importance of effective contingency planning and the need to communicate and work with all interested parties. Previously, the tragic experience of BSE, with the subsequent creation of the Food Standards Agency and Lord Phillips' BSE Inquiry report, radically changed perceptions of the human health risks associated with the food chain. Elsewhere there have been extensive, scientifically underpinned, assessments in recent years of other important elements in the animal health picture – disease surveillance, bovine TB, and the threat from rabies, amongst others.

1.17   The Government now needs an overall strategic approach, drawing on the inquiry reports and on discussions with a wide range of stakeholders. These have begun. The Government will include a brief progress report on the development of the Animal Health and Welfare Strategy in the Strategy for Sustainable Farming and Food published later this year. Regard will also need to be had to the developing EU regulatory framework within which the UK must work.

Other inquiries

1.18   There have been a number of other inquiry processes as a result of the 2001 outbreak. These include:

- The National Audit Office's report on "The 2001 Outbreak of Foot-and-Mouth Disease" published on 21 June 2001, and followed by an examination by the Public Accounts Committee of Defra's Accounting Officer. The Public Accounts Committee's report is awaited and the Government will respond to it in the normal way. The Government welcomes the recommendations made in the National Audit Office's report, which the Lessons Learned and Royal Society reports largely echo. Cross references in Annex I of this response make it clear where action to implement Lessons Learned or Royal Society recommendations also addresses a recommendation made by the National Audit Office.

- Examination of witnesses by the Environment, Food and Rural Affairs Select Committee of the House of Commons in their report "The Impact of Foot-and-Mouth Disease".

- Local inquiries like those by Devon, Shropshire, Gloucestershire, Northumberland and Cumbria County Councils have provided a valuable local perspective. The Government has noted carefully the findings of these inquiries, many of which are reflected in the recommendations of the Lessons Learned and Royal Society reports.

- The Scottish Executive will be responding to the Royal Society of Edinburgh's report on the outbreak in Scotland. In Wales the National Assembly's Agriculture and Rural Development Committee conducted a scrutiny of Ministers and officials and in Northern Ireland PriceWaterhouseCoopers were commissioned to carry out a study of the outbreak there.

- A Temporary Committee established by the European Parliament to look at the FMD outbreak throughout the European Union as a whole, whose report the Parliament is expected to vote on before the end of the year.

- Three EU Food and Veterinary Missions to observe the UK response to FMD; and an EU Financial Audit to examine the UK claim on the EU Veterinary Fund, the report of which is due next year. The European Court of Auditors are also carrying out an audit of FMD.

A new department: the rural economy

1.19   An important theme of the Lessons Learned report is the need to ensure that all the consequences of control of exotic animal diseases for the country as a whole are fully considered. A fundamental difference in the way the Government approached the delivery of rural economic and social policy was signalled by the creation of Defra, one of whose central pillars is the whole rural affairs agenda. This elevation of rural policy, with the first Government Minister for Rural Affairs, reflects the fact – confirmed by the FMD experience – that the rural economy is not a synonym for agriculture, but is now a complex mixed economy in which food production, tourism and recreation, and public and private services, are all important strands.

1.20   The impact of FMD and the measures taken to control it on the wider rural economy – tourism in particular – brought these interrelationships into sharp relief. Defra's objective for rural policy is to enhance opportunity and tackle social exclusion in rural areas, with specific targets to reduce the gap in productivity between the least well performing rural areas and the English median, and improve the accessibility of services for rural people. A sustainable, diverse, modern and adaptable farming industry – another Defra objective – will remain one important element in maintaining sustainable, prosperous and inclusive rural communities.

1.21   The Government is working to embed the needs of rural areas firmly within the mainstream of Government policy by:

- delivery on the Rural White Paper (2000) commitments;

- scrutinising all domestic policies for their consequences for rural people ("rural proofing");

- setting up a Cabinet Sub-Committee for Rural Renewal; and

- appointing Rural Directors in each regional Government Office.

1.22   Defra has also established the Rural Affairs Forum for England to enable the views of those who live and work in, or visit, rural England to inform policy-making. There are 8 regional Rural Affairs Forums in the English regions.

1.23   In Wales, the National Assembly has broad powers and responsibilities to assist rural areas. Since the outbreak in 2001 it has been working with Wales Rural Partnership and supporting the rural community. The Welsh Assembly Government has also strengthened its focus on delivering integrated actions to help rural areas by establishing a Cabinet Committee on the regeneration of rural Wales.

A new department: new ways of working

1.24   As a new department, Defra is committed to – and demonstrating – new ways of working. The experience of early 2001 showed all too strongly the deep connections between the livestock industry and animal health, and wider rural society and the environment. Defra's commitment to sustainable development means recognising those interdependencies in the preparation of the new Animal Health and Welfare Strategy, both in the way the Department prepares it, the people and interests it consults, and the policy approach that results.

1.25   Dr Anderson showed where Defra needed to change and develop to strengthen its delivery capability and modernise the way it goes about its business. He highlighted a culture in Defra which was predisposed to decision-taking by committee with an associated fear of risk-taking and suggested that a reappraisal of prevailing attitudes and behaviours within Defra would be beneficial.

1.26   Defra's ambitious reform programme will address the issues identified in the FMD reports. It will build on the strengths of Defra's predecessor departments and create an organisation which can deal robustly and effectively with its day-to-day business and with emergencies.

1.27   Dr Anderson identified the key areas to consider under three headings: systems, speed and science. Defra has action already in hand under each. But work remains to be done. The following sections summarise the key elements of Defra's programme of work under these headings.

1.28   **Systems**

- Defra is publishing a new and updated Contingency Plan to cover animal disease emergencies; it will develop and test this regularly, involving a wide range of internal and external stakeholders. Defra is consulting on and developing a "decision tree", setting out the criteria by which the Government would make choices between different control strategies during an outbreak;

- a more consistent and systematic approach to risk management is being promoted within Defra, outlined in its Risk Management Strategy published in April 2002.

- Defra has begun the next phase of the change programme which will strengthen its connection to its customers and its focus on service and front line delivery, following a strategic review of the Department carried out jointly with the Office of Public Services Reform;

- integrated corporate IT systems are being developed to provide a strong platform for identifying and tracing animals. This will provide a sound basis for a strengthened and tested disease control information system which provides accurate information, quickly, in a disease outbreak;

- Defra is strengthening its approach to project and programme management, using outside experts to help plan key new policy projects (e.g. on animal movements) and promote skills transfer;

- Defra is closely engaged with the development by the Civil Contingencies Secretariat of the Government's wider emergency response capability, and is working with its representatives in Government Offices to ensure an outward facing and interdepartmental approach to emergency response;

- Defra is reviewing its senior management skills to ensure all its senior managers are well equipped to work within its new style and remit;

- to improve Defra's communication with stakeholders and the general public, an extensive programme of media training – teaching Defra officials and vets across the organisation how to do regional television and radio interviews to a professional standard – is being carried out.

1.29   **Speed**

- Defra has put new arrangements in place to ensure the immediate transmission of information on suspect cases to key stakeholders;

- there are clear plans for roles and responsibilities in a disease outbreak, at operational, tactical and strategic levels, so that officials can make decisions at the right levels quickly;

- the Emergency Preparedness Programme will consider how Defra can better exploit IT and telecommunications systems to speed up communications in the field and cut out communication blockages;

- there will be evaluation, both internal and external, of the simulation exercises from the end of the year with special reference to speed of response.

1.30   **Science**

- a new Science Advisory Group will keep risk issues under close review when advising the Defra Chief Scientific Advisor (CSA). It will also set up rapid and robust arrangements for advice to the Defra CSA in an emergency;

- the new structures for managing disease outbreaks will ensure that scientific advice informs all policy decisions;

- Defra is planning to ensure a stronger co-ordination between the various science bodies to ensure the maximum benefit from research funds, and that the necessary funds are targeted on the key problems;

1.31 Defra therefore has in hand a major programme of work which will reform and speed up the way it goes about its business, and specifically in relation to animal disease emergencies.

A modern State Veterinary Service

1.32 The State Veterinary Service (SVS) is the Government's front line force in responding to disease emergencies. It has a long history of achievement and a world class reputation for professionalism and commitment. The SVS will be building on these professional strengths, and the deep commitment of its staff, and playing its full part in the wider modernisation of Defra. The SVS will work closely with veterinary colleagues in the Veterinary Directorate of the Animal Health and Welfare Directorate General who are charged with policy responsibility. Whilst there have been problems of resources and recruitment into the SVS the Government is committed to maintaining a strong and effective SVS capable of meeting the challenge set out in this response – and some of the recruitment is now taking place. However, there are growing demands on the SVS as well as competing priorities elsewhere in Defra and the Department may need to make some difficult choices on resource allocation.

1.33 Specific action includes:

- Business processes and ways of working across the SVS are being tackled in a wide ranging change programme aimed at a) increasing emphasis on delivery and b) meeting internal and external customer requirements, and open sharing of information;

- A new Disease Control System is being developed to improve the quality of key information required in disease outbreaks;

- stronger links are being forged between the SVS and policy teams to ensure operational issues are taken fully into account as policy is developed, and with Defra's other field operations, over issues such as increased sharing of accommodation and other common services;

- the SVS relationship with private vets is undergoing a comprehensive review to ensure greater clarity and more robust arrangements. This will include improved training, communication, and the possibility of providing a contingency reserve;

- Divisional Veterinary Managers (DVMs) are reinforcing their links with local stakeholders, especially local authorities, and engaging them in the simulation exercises for the new Contingency Plan;

- stronger links are being forged with the Government Office network and the new Government News Network;

- all the DVMs are taking part in the new Defra-wide training programme to strengthen the Department's capacity to deliver change, and to build a stronger more unified senior management;

- work is underway to draw up a new IT investment strategy for the SVS which will speed up process reforms, raise skill levels and the SVS's capacity to exploit new IT technologies, increase efficiency and improve performance;

- a new Board of Management, including representatives of the devolved administrations, will be responsible for agreeing business plans and monitoring performance.

1.34 In these and other ways, the SVS will be an integrated part of the wider Department, working more closely with its Defra and Devolved Administration delivery partners and outside stakeholders to deliver its specialised and professional services.

The Devolved Administrations

1.35   The inquiry reports covered Great Britain. As the Government retained disease control powers in Wales during the 2001 FMD outbreak, this response is being made jointly with the Welsh Assembly Government. Reflecting its accountability on animal health matters to the Scottish Parliament, the Scottish Executive is making its own response to the inquiries. However, it has been associated with the preparation of this response reflecting the GB wide nature of some of the recommendations and the close co-operation which exists between the GB Rural Affairs departments.

1.36   Animal disease outbreaks are no respecters of boundaries. That is why the three GB Rural Affairs departments are working closely together on the development of contingency plans and on planning how best to address any cross border issues that might arise, so as to ensure that any outbreak can be tackled seamlessly. The Animal Health and Welfare Strategy is also being drawn up on a GB basis.

1.37   The Welsh devolution settlement devolved certain animal health powers to the Assembly (such as those which relate to the control of TB) but not others, including those relating to the control of FMD. During the outbreak this did not sit comfortably with Assembly Ministers' accountability to the people of Wales. The Government is therefore in discussion with the Welsh Assembly Government on the case for devolving further powers to it to deal with all future outbreaks of animal disease in Wales.

SECTION 2:   A STRONGER FRAMEWORK FOR EMERGENCY PREPAREDNESS

2.1   Contingency planning

Government-wide framework for contingency planning

2.1.1   The Civil Contingencies Secretariat was set up in July 2001 in recognition of the need to improve and co-ordinate the UK's contingency planning and to help strengthen the UK's resilience at every level to disruptive challenges of the kind seen in the fuel protests, the floods in the winter of 2000 and the FMD outbreak.

2.1.2   Its purpose is to work with others to improve planning for, dealing with and learning lessons from large scale emergencies and disasters. It also leads the Government's horizon scanning activity to identify and assess potential and imminent disruptive challenges to the UK, whatever their source.

2.1.3   It provides integrated planning and thinking, as well as co-ordination of action across departments and others whom Government needs to involve. It reflects the fact that whilst individual Government departments have their own contingency plans, significant emergencies rarely follow departmental boundaries. A central Secretariat is well placed to deliver this co-ordination.

2.1.4   The Secretariat's key tasks are to lead the delivery of improved resilience to disruption across Government and the public sector, including ensuring that core response capabilities are developed and that Government can continue to function and deliver public services during crises; to identify potential challenges and their impacts; to help departments pre-empt them or handle them; and to manage any necessary co-ordination machinery.

2.1.5   The Secretariat's plans for emergencies and its liaison within Government enable departments' own contingency plans to operate within a wider framework. The Food Standards Agency is part of that framework, which means any new or emerging food safety risk issues will be dealt with effectively during a crisis. In future the European Food Safety Authority will also provide an overview of risk, at the European level, to the European Commission.

2.1.6   Local authorities have a key role to play and the Secretariat will be placing additional emphasis on working with local authorities and their emergency planners to ensure that the UK's contingency planning is as robust as possible. The Secretariat will work to build successful and mutually beneficial relationships with local authorities. There are also plans to enhance the capacity of Government Offices from 2003, establishing dedicated contingency planning teams in each region. These will provide a valuable resource in any future outbreak.

Developing the Contingency Plan

2.1.7   An outbreak of FMD on the scale the country experienced in 2001 will always involve massive disruption to the agricultural sector and the wider rural economy, substantial cost and the need for the large-scale mobilisation of resources, including people, equipment and transport. There will inevitably be suffering and loss for those who are affected directly and there will be many more whose lives are disrupted. No contingency plan, however effective and well rehearsed, can avoid that. What the Government is determined to do is to ensure that the suffering and disruption is kept to a minimum, and that the outbreak is tackled with speed and vigour. These overall aims are reflected in Defra's work on contingency planning, described below and in Section 4.2.

2.1.8   Since the 2001 epidemic much work within Defra has gone into developing contingency planning for an outbreak of FMD. Similar work has been taking place in Scotland and Wales and there is close liaison not only on the development of the plans but also in planning how cross border issues that might arise should be best addressed. Existing contingency plans for other exotic diseases are also being reviewed and updated. The last version of the FMD interim Contingency Plan was placed on the Defra website on 3 July for consultation. A revised version of the FMD Contingency Plan appears on the Defra website to coincide with the publication of this response. This builds on the interim Plan and provides the administrative framework for local office contingency plans and detailed veterinary instructions. A new division in the State Veterinary Service is now working to keep the plan as a living document, updating and augmenting it as policies are developed and exercises completed.

2.1.9   The Contingency Plan is being developed in modules. The core modules will cover the strategic level of the command structure, the establishment of a national disease control centre responsible for reporting disease and the administration, liaison and communication structures that are necessary to support the veterinary effort and disease control at a national level. It will also cover the setting up and expansion of local disease control centres with arrangements for engaging additional veterinary, technical and administrative staff. Revised arrangements for initiating the FMD disease control operation will form another module and additional modules will be prepared for other diseases or groups of diseases depending on the species affected or the way in which the disease spreads.

2.1.10   Defra will also develop modules to cover wider aspects of dealing with a disease outbreak. These will include the development of a "procurement package" to ensure that all staff have immediately available to them guidance on cost effective procurement and draft model contracts. Similarly a financial package will provide instruction and guidance to those brought in to work on finance and compensation. The recruitment and management of staff form another module. Each local office also maintains its own detailed contingency plan which complements the nationally agreed disease control structures and arrangements for increasing staff with local contact lists and other locally relevant information.

Implementing policies

2.1.11   Contingency plans are not only concerned with operational issues. They reflect and build on disease control policies. The current Contingency Plan is based on the current disease control policies which include targets for slaughter on infected premises, implementation of a GB wide movement standstill of susceptible livestock, withdrawal of export licences for animals and animal products and disposal by incineration followed by disposal by rendering. If policies change, plans will be reviewed and amended accordingly. Arrangements for emergency vaccination are being further developed building on those set up during the 2001 outbreak.

Involving others

2.1.12   The inquiries emphasised the importance of the Contingency Plan being available to all those who would be involved, so that all fully understand their roles in the event of an outbreak of animal disease. The Contingency Plan is therefore being developed with input from stakeholders and will continue to be available on the Defra website for information and comments. But the Government is also determined to ensure that all those involved as operational partners (both locally and nationally) should understand their roles and be able to contribute to developing the plan. In particular in the light of the importance of the role of local authorities in controlling animal disease, Divisional Veterinary Managers will seek to strengthen existing contacts with the local authority emergency planning officers and trading standards officers through ongoing work on movement licensing and by meetings and exercises. Working with local authorities will also allow good use to be made of their unrivalled local knowledge and ground intelligence.

2.1.13   Detailed work on some modules of the Contingency Plan also requires the close involvement of interested parties. Work on disposal options is particularly important in the light of the concerns that carcass disposal generated last year. Discussions are under way with the United Kingdom Renderers

Association and the Environmental Services Association to investigate and develop the most effective arrangements for carcass movement and disposal. Disposal plans must also be set in the context of the current and developing legislative framework and will therefore involve those responsible for waste disposal policies and, as the enforcement body, the Environment Agency.

Training and Exercises

2.1.14   Since the last confirmed case of FMD was reported on 30 September 2001, there have been over 90 reports of FMD type conditions in farm animals. Experienced State Veterinary Service vets have quickly cleared the great majority of these on clinical investigation and without need for laboratory testing. However in three cases there has been enough doubt in the vets' minds for samples to be taken for laboratory testing. This has led to restrictions being placed within an 8km radius of each of the suspect premises and has provided the opportunity to exercise the initial notification and alert procedures in the interim Contingency Plan. The lessons learned from the suspect cases have led to revisions to the notification processes. However, in recognition that the full range of contingency measures needs to be tested regularly a programme of exercises is being planned. This will provide training for those involved in dealing with an outbreak as well as testing the efficacy of the plans.

2.1.15   The development of contingency plans requires the training of all staff involved and practice in implementation to check that the plans work. Separate elements of the plans will be tested and independently assessed to ensure a common understanding and application of the arrangements is achieved across the country and to check the links between local and central offices and that all the national structures operate effectively. Defra will involve stakeholders in developing and exercising these plans. Centrally run exercises in local offices and in the national centre will take place before the end of the year.

Parliamentary debate

2.1.16   The inquiries recommended that Parliament should debate and confirm the contingency plans either as a framework at the outset or as a complete document on a regular basis. It is clearly important that there should be understanding of the plans at all levels. The Government will therefore be providing the plans to the Select Committee on Environment, Food and Rural Affairs and bringing them to Parliament once further work and testing has taken place.

Welsh Assembly Contingency Planning

2.1.17   The Welsh Assembly Government has developed its own interim contingency plan in conjunction with partners and stakeholders. This has been subject to public consultation which ended in October. There is close liaison between Defra and the Welsh Assembly Government to ensure consistency of approach regarding contingency planning, with joint training and exercises planned for the future.

2.2   Communications

2.2.1   The Government agrees with the principles of good communications set out in the Lessons Learned report. Defra's Communications Directorate aims to improve communications at all levels internally and externally.

2.2.2   Defra's overall communications aims are:

- to communicate accurate and relevant information in a way that is timely, responsive and appropriately targeted, using all available tools;

- to be clear, consistent and coherent in all communications and to strive for a better shared understanding of issues;

- to promote factually the work of Defra and prevent an information vacuum on any Defra policy issue; and

- to anticipate where events are going next and to have a backup plan.

2.2.3   Experience, especially in the early stages of the 2001 outbreak, highlighted the urgent need for improvements in various aspects of communications. In particular, for more co-ordination and explanation of the often very complex technical information involved; ways of keeping all staff across the organisation better and more quickly informed and the limitations of this when communicating with staff spending most of their time out of the office; and the need for better ways of working with regional media. These issues were addressed, as much as possible, during the outbreak, but work has continued to improve communications throughout Defra, both in "peacetime" and to explore and set up new ways of working in any future crisis. More detail is provided in Section 4.2.

2.3   Risk management

2.3.1   Defra published its Risk Management Strategy in April 2002. This sets out the principles that will apply and the main processes that Defra will use when dealing with risk and uncertainty throughout the Department. It clearly states the desire to move to an environment of 'No Surprises', to recognise more widely that risk is about threat *and* opportunity and that Defra must take calculated risks if it is to release innovation and improve performance.

2.3.2   Senior managers must drive much of the impetus for change and risk is now more formally on the Defra Management Board's agenda, not only in terms of reviewing the top threats (one of which is the risk of a major animal health crisis) but also in receiving periodic snapshots of the portfolio of risk that the whole Department is carrying, built up from risk registers in each Directorate and Executive Agency. This will help drive risk awareness and improved risk management lower down in the organisation. In all of this, the need to improve public trust in Defra's advice and management is recognised and the Department is considering ways of monitoring improvements.

2.3.3   Defra also needs to have the trust of its own staff and to develop a climate in which it is OK to give bad news. A survey of staff in Summer 2002 is providing key information on where the Department is, particularly on: the degree of encouragement to challenge accepted ways of doing things; the degree of encouragement to identify and manage risks; the degree of blame when decisions are taken and things 'go wrong'; the relationships with managers; and the leadership of the Board. Defra will then make clear plans to tackle the priority areas.

2.3.4   There is a central Government dimension for each department's handling of risk. Defra has worked closely with the Prime Minister's Strategy Unit in its Risk and Uncertainty project. Defra welcomes the Unit's recommendations and will work with them in their proposed two-year change programme, aimed at improving Government's capability to handle risk and uncertainty.

2.4   Legislative framework

International rules – the OIE

2.4.1   The Office International des Epizooties (OIE) is an international animal health organisation that sets guidelines for international trade and laboratory standards for the control of disease or to provide health guarantees in respect of trade. New standards are ratified annually at the OIE General Session by all OIE member states. It monitors the international animal health situation and provides expertise in animal diseases and their diagnosis through OIE designated reference laboratories. The UK, like all EU Member States, is a member of the OIE and the rules it is subject to, both for intra-Community trade and trade with non-EU countries, respect the OIE guidelines.

2.4.2   The OIE classifies diseases in terms of their economic importance and severity and member countries are obliged to notify the OIE immediately, and through it the international community, of outbreaks of those diseases judged to be most important (List A diseases). FMD is a list A disease and because of its importance, the OIE accords countries animal health status in respect of FMD. There are three classifications:

- FMD free country or zone where vaccination is not practised (the highest in terms of international trade)

- FMD free country or zone where vaccination is practised

- FMD infected country

2.4.3   If a country loses the status of 'FMD free country or zone where vaccination is not practised' due to an outbreak, it can regain this status:

- after a slaughter policy: when there have been no cases of FMD for at least 3 months;

- after a policy of emergency vaccination followed by slaughter: when there have been no cases of FMD for at least 3 months since the last vaccinated animal was slaughtered;

- if animals are vaccinated and allowed to live: 6 months since the last case of FMD or since the last animal was vaccinated must elapse.

2.4.4   The member country also has to demonstrate to the OIE in all these cases that it has eradicated the disease and, in particular, that it has carried out adequate serological surveillance and applied appropriate controls to convince them that this is the case. This includes testing vaccinated animals to show they are not infected.

2.4.5   The Royal Society recommended that Defra should consult other member states to ensure that the OIE is appropriately constituted to validate new diagnostic techniques and reagents as rapidly as possible and that OIE reference laboratories are supported politically and financially so they can better undertake their national and international obligations, including the development of diagnostic tests. The Government accepts this recommendation. The OIE Standards Commission is the existing mechanism for evaluating diagnostic tests and reagents and agreeing to their use. Whilst rapid validation of new techniques is desirable, the need for detailed and evidence based assessment means that member state laboratories must do preparatory work, and these rely on their host country's support. The Government will continue to support OIE reference laboratories such as the Institute for Animal Health at Pirbright so that they can fully meet their obligations and contribute to this process.

European Community legislation – Directive 85/511

2.4.6   The UK is subject to European Union rules for the control of exotic diseases such as FMD, Classical and African Swine Fever and Bluetongue, and for trade between Member States and between the Community and third countries, aimed at protecting and maintaining the EU's disease free status. These are set down in EU legislative instruments which are adopted by the Commission or Council after agreement by the Member States. As far as FMD is concerned, EU policy since 1992 has been based on all Member States *being FMD free without vaccination* and this is reflected in the FMD control Directive 85/511/EEC which requires Member States to stamp out disease. The Directive makes provision for governments to use emergency vaccination in an outbreak but vaccination has to take place under terms agreed by the Commission and the Member States.

2.4.7   Directive 85/511/EEC lays down the minimum procedures which a Member State must follow when an outbreak of FMD occurs on its territory. Member States may also take measures additional to those in the Directive.

2.4.8   The UK Government appreciates the co-operation it received from the European Commission and other Member States and the speed with which amending Decisions were taken to Community law which were necessary for the eradication of disease and the restoration of intra-Community trade once it had been eradicated. It will ensure that discussion of the Commission's proposals for a revision of Directive 85/511 are informed by its own experiences and lessons learned during the 2001 FMD epidemic as well as the recommendations of the FMD inquiries. The European Parliament is expected to adopt the report of its Temporary Committee on FMD in December. This is likely to cover similar ground to the findings of the UK inquiries, including use of emergency vaccination as a control measure and tighter import controls.

Domestic legislation – the Animal Health Act

2.4.9   In Great Britain the Animal Health Act 1981 provides the legal basis to control animal diseases. Within GB, the execution of the powers laid down in this legislation rests, in varying degrees, with Devolved Administrations in Scotland and Wales. Animal health is fully devolved to the Scottish Parliament, which has primary and secondary legislative responsibility. Separate but parallel legislation applies to Northern Ireland, reflecting its status as a separate epidemiological unit from GB, and its need to take account of rules applying in the Irish Republic.

2.4.10   The 1981 Animal Health Act and the secondary legislation made under it give Ministers in Great Britain broad powers to deal with disease outbreaks such as FMD. These powers proved adequate to implement the disease control strategies used during the 2001 outbreak. In particular, the Act provided a legal basis for the slaughter of FMD infected animals, animals suspected of being infected, animals which in some way have been in contact with affected animals, and animals which appear to the Minister to have been in any way exposed to the infection of FMD. These powers were used to carry out culling on infected premises, and of animals classed as "dangerous contacts". On the basis of veterinary advice that such animals would have been exposed to FMD infection, the powers were also used to cull animals on contiguous premises and (in Cumbria and Southern Scotland) in a 3km zone around infected premises.

2.4.11   The Government notes the finding of the Lessons Learned Inquiry that during the 2001 epidemic, the animal health legislative framework was not "robust, unambiguous and fit for purpose". The Government does not consider the existing Animal Health Act powers to be ambiguous. For example during the 2001 outbreak, the courts upheld the legality of the contiguous cull (MAFF v Winslade), one of the most contentious areas of policy. However, the Government welcomes the recommendation in the Lessons Learned report that the Government should make provision for pre-emptive culling.

2.4.12   The Government believes that its Animal Health Bill helps to meet some of the inquiry recommendations[1]. The Bill contains additional powers which would enable the Government to employ pre-emptive culling strategies where appropriate, alongside clearer powers of entry for the purposes of testing, culling and vaccination. The Bill would also allow a contiguous cull even where it could be argued that animals on contiguous premises had not been exposed to the disease, and therefore furthers the clarity of the law, which the Lessons Learned Inquiry considered so important.

2.4.13   The Government's view is that this Bill should become law as soon as possible, as the measures provided by the Bill are a response to the threat of a future outbreak of disease. The Government believes these powers would enable it to contain disease more effectively and eradicate it more quickly. The

---

[1] The Bill before the Westminster Parliament applies to England and Wales only; separate legislation is being prepared for consideration by the Scottish Parliament.

Government considers that enactment of the Bill would address the concerns expressed by the Lessons Learned Inquiry that animal health legislation should be robust and fit for the purpose.

2.4.14   The Lessons Learned Inquiry suggested that there might be a more general review of the Animal Health legislation. The Government agrees with this, and will address the scope and nature of future legislation next year following publication of the Animal Health and Welfare Strategy. This is likely to involve rationalisation of existing regulation, covering issues such as encouraging better biosecurity, harmonising systems of compensation and risk sharing as between industry and the taxpayer.

2.5   Research

2.5.1   The Government is aware of the importance of sound science underpinning the formation and application of policy. It was for that reason that the Royal Society was asked to review the scientific questions that underlie animal disease policy. Their report represents an important contribution to the policy process.

Investment and co-ordination of research

2.5.2   The Royal Society rightly stresses the importance of investing in research – and surveillance and monitoring – to underpin the development and application of Government policies. The Government accepts the need to increase spending in this area and will strengthen co-ordination across funders, including EU funded research. The key issues identified by the Royal Society are the prioritisation and co-ordination of funders' work so as to maximise the impact of scientific endeavour. This will inform the amount of public funding needed.

Research funding

2.5.3   The Royal Society summarises the interest and involvement of a number of Government funders – and also the Wellcome Trust and the Animal Health Trust – in supporting scientific programmes. Together, these represent a substantial investment in understanding and dealing with infectious diseases of livestock. Annex II sets out the current position of the major funders and includes a note on infrastructure matters. This covers Defra, the Biotechnology and Biological Sciences Research Council (BBSRC), the Department for International Development, the Scottish Executive, Northern Ireland and the Wellcome Trust. The analysis shows that there continues to be a range of new and important research work in farm animal diseases as well as farm animal welfare.

2.5.4   The Government is committed to funding necessary research into animal disease and to increasing spending on animal disease research. But further work is needed to decide if it is justified to invest £250m of new money over the next ten years. It is essential that research needs are analysed and work is well in hand to do this, taking account of the research areas identified by the Royal Society. The Government's research priorities will be formulated within Defra's Animal Health and Welfare Strategy, taking account of work that will rightly be undertaken on an EU or international basis (see below). Government funders are now working through their spending review settlements. Whilst different funders have different settlements, the total Research and Development programme expenditure for each will at least be protected in real terms at the levels of the previous spending round throughout the years to 2005/6. Appropriate levels of funding will then be allocated to animal disease research within the settlement amounts.

Research co-ordination

2.5.5   The Royal Society makes a strong case for better co-ordination of research effort by the main funders and the Government accepts that more could and should be done to increase the linkages. There are valid distinctions between the nature of that research – for example strategic and applied strategic research needed and funded by Government departments – and the more speculative "blue skies" research carried out at Research Council Institutes and Universities. It is also true that the roles of Research and Development and the effort on surveillance and monitoring can have complementary roles.

2.5.6   Soon after the publication of the Royal Society report, an interdepartmental group was tasked to consider these aspects. The Government could adopt a number of approaches, from the co-ordinating Committee approach taken by Government for its research work on transmissible spongiform encephalopathies, to a more fundamental option involving a root-and-branch rebrigading of all current scientific activity on infectious animal diseases. Several models will lie between these ones and the Government plans to pursue and consult on these arrangements. It will do this in the light of the current review of Defra's Science-based Executive Agencies and the recent review of the Institute for Animal Health at Pirbright by Professor Keith Gull. In any new arrangements for strengthened co-ordination, the Government must preserve a number of features of the way in which it currently develops research requirements – notably through access to independent advice; the application of peer review; and appropriate elements of open competition in the procurement of research.

European research

2.5.7   The Government agrees that there is a need to co-ordinate research efforts into livestock diseases across Europe and that the Community should fund this to a common agenda. The EU's Framework Programmes for research, technology and development have long provided a number of ways of assisting in both funding for research into livestock diseases; and for collaborative research activities across the Community and increasingly with its associated states and others such as Switzerland, Hungary, Poland, Australia and the USA. A successful example is Transmissible Spongiform Encephalopathies (TSE) research in which some €35m was set aside under Framework Programme 4 to establish projects and networks. That programme is being taken forward under the current programme (Framework Programme 5) bringing total funding to €85m. UK research teams feature prominently.

2.5.8   The Government is keen to foster similar successful research into animal health issues at the European level. Framework Programme 6 runs from 2002-2006 and provides mechanisms for fostering co-ordination through the European Research Area concept. Priority thematic areas include life sciences, genomics and biotechnology for health (€2255m) and food quality and safety (€685m). An additional €160m has been allocated for EU policy development, including specific provision for research into new and more environmentally friendly production methods to improve animal health and welfare including research on animal diseases and the development of vaccines. The Veterinary Laboratories Agency and the Institute for Animal Health at Pirbright as well as a number of other UK institutions working in the animal health area are actively involved in proposals for funding through Framework Programme 6.

Veterinary teaching and research

2.5.9   The Government accepts that veterinary teaching and research needs additional funding and will allocate an additional £25m over the next five years.

2.5.10   Vets play a crucial role in the health and welfare of animals both in clinical practice and in research, particularly clinical veterinary research both into individual animal care and the health of animal populations. Their effectiveness can only be sustained by ensuring that veterinary science has sufficient and appropriate research and teaching capacity. The Selborne report (1997) was commissioned by the Royal College of Veterinary Surgeons to address the problem that too few people with veterinary qualifications were adopting research careers and that the funding arrangements for clinical veterinary teaching needed improving.

2.5.11   Defra has been concerned for some years about the need to develop capacity for post-graduate centres of research excellence in the Veterinary schools. To these ends, Defra has supported Veterinary Fellowships at the Universities of Cambridge, Liverpool and Edinburgh with a total planned spend of £3.9m since the programme began in 1999. As a further addition to this important capacity building – and in the light of the report by Lord Selborne – Defra is committing further funds to a new initiative involving the Higher Education Funding Council for England and with match-funding from the Wellcome Trust to invest in veterinary research and teaching with these aims in mind. The details of this programme, involving a £25m investment by Government over the next 5 years, with a matching £25m from the Trust, were announced by Ministers on 23rd July 2002. The funders are consulting with the Royal College of Veterinary Surgeons on how to deploy these funds to maximum effect.

Independent advice

2.5.12   The Lessons Learned report recommends that Defra's Chief Scientific Adviser (CSA) maintains a properly constituted committee to advise in an emergency on the scientific aspects of disease control. This should cover horizon-scanning and emerging risks. Defra has set up a new Science Advisory Group to advise the Defra CSA on all matters associated with science and risk issues. This will become a Non-Departmental Public Body called the Science Advisory Council next year. A subgroup of this body will be activated upon confirmation of any outbreak of an infectious disease of animals to advise the Defra CSA on scientific issues, as a high level technical advisory committee. The subgroup will consist of experts from outside Government who will be able to provide a rapid response to technical and scientific issues raised by such an outbreak. The Defra CSA will chair this committee and it will involve academics and senior officials from the relevant departments (including the Government's CSA, the Department of Health, and the Ministry of Defence and the Cabinet Office Civil Contingencies Secretariat) and other EU experts.

2.5.13   The Government agrees with the Lessons Learned report which notes that such a committee needs to give particular attention to the recommendations on the use of Scientific Advisory Committees, as referred to in the report of the BSE Inquiry of 2000 (page 91). The Defra CSA recognises the importance of independent advice to support the scientific input to policy decisions on animal disease control. He will ensure that the independent Science Advisory Council is properly constituted on "Phillips" principles (as set out in the report of the BSE Inquiry), and in the light of the Office of Science and Technology's Code on the Conduct of Scientific Advisory Committees.

2.5.14   The Royal Society endorses the proposals by the Policy Commission on the Future of Farming and Food for a new Priorities Board on Farming and Food Chain Research, closely involving industry and other stakeholder interests. Defra has accepted these proposals and is taking them forward separately.

Applied research unit

2.5.15   The Royal Society proposes that Defra should establish an applied research unit on livestock management practices to undertake or commission research on the design of effective biosecurity measures against infectious diseases, as well as livestock management structures and practices that improve animal health in terms of infectious diseases.

2.5.16   There is a Unit within the Science Directorate of Defra whose research commissioning remit covers these and related themes. The Unit runs collaborative programmes with the Scottish Executive. The Government recognises that more needs to be done to secure the health of UK livestock. It has deployed resources for research to diagnose and respond to exotic microbial infections such as FMD. The Veterinary Laboratories Agency and the Institute for Animal Health at Pirbright are examining diagnosis and prophylaxis. Defra and other funders also support research into livestock management practices which is designed to improve the ability of farm animals to resist infectious disease challenge. Current research in pursuit of these aims totals some £10.5m per year.

SECTION 3:   STRENGTHENING DISEASE PREVENTION

3.1   International intelligence and import controls

3.1.1   Reports from sources such as the Office International des Epizooties (OIE) and notifications from the European Commission about the animal health status of other countries are monitored and collated by Defra and are used to identify significant animal disease outbreaks within the EU and worldwide. This information gathering enables evaluation of disease risks and implementation of regulatory controls in the UK. Defra is developing an electronic information management system to manage its recording of information better, streamline its response to disease incidence in countries from which the UK imports animals and products and provide a mapping facility to aid assessment of disease spread across national borders.

3.1.2   The Royal Society recommends an EU wide risk assessment unit and centralised database on surveillance and disease data and a review of the bodies that provide early warning of animal disease threats. These are largely matters for the bodies in question but the Government will support international efforts to improve data collection and reporting. The OIE is actively promoting animal disease reporting, animal health information dissemination and epidemiological surveillance and has, on behalf of the Food and Agriculture Organisation (FAO), OIE and World Health Organisation (WHO), assumed responsibility for the collection of information on the animal health situation worldwide, seeking input from all countries which are members of at least one of the three organisations.

3.1.3   As recommended by both inquiries, the Government is taking action to tackle illegal meat imports. Defra is responsible for co-ordinating the activities listed in the Action Plan published in March 2002 (see www.defra.gov.uk/animalh/illegali).

3.1.4   Better prevention and detection of illegal imports is dependent on:

- Effective publicity of the country's import rules and reasons for them;

- Clear and simple rules to aid compliance and enforcement;

- Effective deterrence measures;

- Effective methods of detection; and

- Good intelligence.

3.1.5   All these are covered by the Government's Action Plan. The House of Commons Environment Food and Rural Affairs Committee in its Seventh report of session 2001-02 (to examine the adequacy of this plan) commented 'we have generally been impressed with the speed with which Government and stakeholders have acted to address the various elements of the plan'.

3.1.6   The Government has already achieved a great deal of progress on the Action Plan. Some of the highlights are:

- The launch of a publicity campaign in July, with the slogan 'Don't bring back more than you bargained for'. This builds on the work started in 2001 to raise public awareness of the potential risks in bringing back illicit products. The campaign has involved the production and distribution of nearly 200,000 information leaflets, 1500 campaign posters and a radio filler. Defra has distributed two videos to airlines, national TV stations and other outlets. Defra is keeping all publicity activities under review.

- The Government has taken action at points of departure through its embassies, to raise awareness of its import rules, including issuing advice with visas.

- The start, on schedule, on 16 September of the pilot into the use of detector dogs. To 25 October, 111 seizures of products of animal origin had been made as a result of detection by the dogs, totalling 701kg, of which 302kg was meat.

- Successful lobbying of the European Commission for tighter rules on personal imports. Under the new rules, which come into force on 1 January 2003, personal imports of meat, meat products, milk and milk products will be prohibited for travellers entering the UK from outside the European Union.

- Improved intelligence gathering and sharing. Information held on a central database has since June been passed to enforcement officers to aid anti-smuggling checks. Defra has also had contact with specialist intelligence units such as the National Criminal Intelligence Service and the Wildlife Criminal Investigation Unit.

- Legislation was amended in May to provide enforcement officers with better powers to search passenger' bags.

3.1.7   Over £3 million is being spent this financial year to implement the measures set out in the Action Plan. Of this, £1.5 million is funding additional enforcement officers at ports and airports. This began in October and is being rolled out to a number of ports and airports. In the first three weeks of working at Felixstowe, over 1 tonne of products of animal origin were seized.

Risk Assessment

3.1.8   The Government is determined to achieve a step-change in its illegal imports controls. It accepts the recommendations of the inquiries and stakeholder interests that these controls must be evidence based. It therefore commissioned a risk analysis to provide an answer to the question:

> *for each specified hazard, what is the probability per year that the importation of meat will result in at least one infection of the specified hazard in the GB livestock population*

3.1.9   Priority is being given to analysing the risk from FMD. The Risk Assessment consists of three modules that calculate:

- the amount of meat that enters GB illegally;

- the amount of this meat that is infected with FMD at point of entry to GB; and

- the probability that this infected meat will result in the infection of susceptible livestock in GB.

3.1.10   This has been a major and complex study from which the Government is now receiving final results which are being peer reviewed with a view to publishing them later this Autumn. The process of collecting the data has filled many gaps in the Government's knowledge of the risks involved and will be very valuable in informing decisions on further action required.

Organisational roles and responsibilities

3.1.11   The Cabinet Office has recently concluded an urgent three month study into the organisation of the Government's controls on imports of animals, fish, plants and their products. It is clear from this that while many things are being done very well, there is definite room for improvement in key areas. The spending review made available £5 million of new money in 2003-04, and £10 million per annum thereafter, to help secure this.

3.1.12   As a result the Government will rapidly move to:

(a)   bring all activity against smuggling of meat, animal products, fish and plant matter together in Customs and Excise. This will be backed by a new dedicated target in Customs for service delivery in this area.

(b) substantially improve co-ordination between the main control agencies, (including Defra, the Food Standards Agency, the Forestry Commission and local authorities) and between these agencies and Customs, under the oversight of a new ministerial group.

3.1.13   The Government recognises there is a strong case for a single agency to oversee all aspects of the management of legal trade. But that is not an immediate proposition. In the immediate period, the Government will aim first to secure a step change in the co-ordination and delivery of local authority inspection of imported foodstuffs and products of animal origin at ports within one year. It will then look hard again at the case for bringing these functions from local authorities into a central agency, or delivering them from other routes.

Future action

3.1.14   In the light of the results of the Risk Assessment and the Cabinet Office study the Government's intention is to develop a revised Action Plan on illegal imports by early in 2003 which will include:

- a longer term enforcement strategy to ensure effective and proportionate checks against illegal imports of animal products and other foodstuffs at ports and airports and inland;

- further development of initiatives on detection (e.g. use of detector dogs) taking account of initial results from pilot studies;

- enhanced and co-ordinated publicity materials, building on the experience of the 2002 campaign.

The Government has allocated additional resources to develop these initiatives. However, it recognises that there is still much to be achieved.

3.2   National Surveillance

3.2.1   Both inquiries recognise the important role that surveillance plays in disease control and preparedness. The primary purpose of the Government carrying out veterinary surveillance is to meet its basic information needs in order to assess and manage risks effectively. That is to minimise as far as possible the probability of adverse effects on public health, trade in animals and animal products, and animal health and welfare. The availability of veterinary surveillance information is therefore an essential requirement in meeting the Government's aim to protect the public's interest in relation to health and ensure high standards of animal health and welfare.

Veterinary surveillance should:

- enable prompt recognition and appropriate response to disease outbreaks;

- enable the effectiveness of control measures for diseases or infections to be assessed;

- enable the early recognition of important trends to inform risk management policies; and

- enable the identification of new potential hazards.

The Review of Veterinary Surveillance carried out by MAFF in 1999-2000 (Meah and Lewis) identified the need for a clear published strategy for veterinary surveillance. Work is now well underway to develop a Government strategy for veterinary surveillance (although interrupted by the epidemics of Classical Swine Fever and FMD). Resources have been made available both for developing the Strategy and putting in place the systems needed to improve data collection and management. The strategy is being developed with stakeholders, and will be issued for consultation later in the year.

3.2.2   The Strategy will build on the strengths and address the weaknesses of the current approach to veterinary surveillance. It will link to public health and food safety surveillance, and deliver better integration with research.

3.2.3   There are five strategic goals:

- to strengthen collaborations between the providers, users and beneficiaries of veterinary surveillance;

- to develop a transparent and open prioritisation process;

- to derive better value from surveillance information and activities;

- to share information more widely; and

- to enhance the quality assurance of outputs.

3.2.4   Farmers, vets, and others in the livestock industry have important roles in surveillance. Defra is also working with the veterinary profession to explore how Local Veterinary Inspectors can most effectively contribute. This includes how they can feedback information on unusual clinical observations, how they can participate in surveys, and how knowledge gained can be fed back to the livestock industry.

3.2.5   The Veterinary Surveillance Strategy will also identify laboratories that have a key role to play in diseases of national importance. The strategy will define the critical linkages required to laboratory service providers such as the Veterinary Laboratories Agency, the Institute for Animal Health and Scottish Agriculture Colleges.

3.2.6   The Veterinary Surveillance Strategy will improve the coverage and integration of animal disease data by making links with data from other sources in Defra and beyond including geographical information data. This will enable the Government to set information about animal disease in the context of the numbers and location of susceptible livestock. Animal populations at particular risk can then be identified and targeted for appropriate prevention and control measures.

3.2.7   The Surveillance Group on Diseases and Infections of Animals was established in 1999 to co-ordinate veterinary surveillance across Government. It reviews key surveillance issues and decides on strategic action. It also provides a network for rapid response when new hazards are identified.

3.2.8   In addition, Defra is currently developing a Geographical Information (GI) strategy which will cover the use of GI across core Defra, its agencies and selected Non-Departmental Public Bodies. The strategy will ensure that GI data and application development activities that could have benefits to more than one business area are managed to deliver maximum benefits to Defra as a whole.

3.3   Movement rules

3.3.1   Since last year's outbreak an animal movement control system has been in place, with a 20 day standstill applying to most movements (though with increasing exemptions). Both inquiries recognised the importance of animal movement controls as part of a disease prevention strategy, alongside other elements such as surveillance, import controls, animal identification and biosecurity. The Lessons Learned Inquiry recommended that the 20 day standstill should remain in place until the Government had carried out a detailed risk assessment and wide-ranging cost-benefit analysis, to balance the disease control benefits against the economic effects on the livestock sector and the wider rural economy. The Royal Society also suggested that the Government should undertake a cost-benefit analysis of various standstill periods.

3.3.2   The Government fully accepts these recommendations, and has commissioned a wide ranging study to inform a decision on the role movement standstills should play in the future. This study has a number of strands:

- an assessment of the risk of FMD strains entering the UK and reaching susceptible livestock. The illegal imports risk assessment will provide this;

- studies to model the potential impact of such an introduction of virus into the UK, comparing a range of variations to the 20 day standstill rule to see which would provide best protection; and

- an economic assessment of the implications of the 20 day standstill and variations to it. This will include the impact on livestock markets and the rural economy generally, as well as on the cattle and sheep sectors.

3.3.3   The main industry organisations have been involved in the design and management of the studies as well as in providing information to those carrying out the work. Defra will bring together results from these separate strands into an integrated cost-benefit analysis and regulatory impact assessment to inform decisions. The studies involved are complex, but the Government intends to draw on emerging findings from the work in framing the movement controls to apply from February 2003, and if necessary the Government will adjust the controls as soon as possible thereafter in the light of the final assessment.

3.3.4   Representatives of all farming organisations have been involved with Defra to try to find the basis for a balanced regime. Some relaxations were introduced for the Autumn regime, particularly relating to breeding animals. However, the Government needs to establish a more permanent system which is widely understood and supported.

3.3.5   The Government believes, based on the scientific, veterinary and other advice available to it, that it will not be appropriate to return to the pre-2001 position in which there were no movement controls whatever applied to cattle or sheep in normal circumstances. It believes that movement controls of some kind will be needed for the long term, given that despite the significant improvements the Government is making, absolute import protection will be impossible to achieve. Defra, the Devolved Administrations and local authorities will work together so that, so far as is possible, movement controls are consistent across Great Britain. The Government is keen to ensure that any such controls are proportionate and practical for farmers, and is confident that the suite of studies now in progress will provide the information and analysis needed to achieve that outcome in consultation with all interested parties.

3.4   Identification and tracing

3.4.1   The aim of the new Livestock Identification Programme, as recommended by the Lessons Learned Inquiry, is to improve the identification and tracing of UK livestock by introducing a single platform of animal information, with electronic identification for individual cattle, sheep and, if required, pigs. This will allow keepers to scan their livestock with a piece of equipment for reading the individual electronic identification device, and then transfer this digital data, either directly, or through an office system, to a central Defra database.

3.4.2   These new methods of livestock identification and tracing will be introduced over the next few years, most probably starting with sheep and goats. Plans are, however, dependent on EU decisions. Recent statements from the European Commission lead the Government to expect proposals on individual sheep and goat identification to be presented to the Council and European Parliament shortly.

3.4.3   In consultation with stakeholders, Defra and the Devolved Administrations will develop new and simpler business processes to make use of the improved ways of keeping individual animal information. They will further rationalise IT systems and data standards established so that accurate animal information can be maintained.

3.4.4   Animal data from a number of databases, including the British Cattle Movement Service, will be consolidated and a data cleansing exercise undertaken. This provides opportunities to rationalise the way similar information is collected and held by Government for a wide range of purposes. Business process change will reduce red tape burdens on producers by providing a central point of contact for collecting information for disease monitoring and control, verification of animal subsidy claims, improved traceability of sheep, goats and potentially pigs, feedback to external stakeholders and improved consumer assurance on quality UK-produced meat. New money has been made available over the next three years for major IT developments necessary to deliver the Livestock Identification programme.

3.5   Biosecurity

3.5.1   Biosecurity has rightly been identified by the two inquiries as a key element of disease control. Biosecurity elements of disease control in an outbreak are covered in Section 4. To a large extent, the prevention of animal disease will rely on the keepers of livestock and promotion of good biosecurity practices.

3.5.2   The Government is conscious of the need to continue progress towards achieving higher standards of biosecurity, and to build on the foundations now in place. This will not only help to protect livestock against a new incursion of exotic disease but also help to control endemic diseases.

3.5.3   The Government regularly issues advice on biosecurity measures in relation to particular species or diseases. This is available on the internet and by direct mailing to known keepers of livestock. Continued funding for research to provide the most up to date information on how to prevent disease transmission will be necessary to underpin the provision of targeted advice. In addition, the Government needs to review the provision of advice in order to determine whether there are more effective ways of getting the message across, and to make it readily accessible to the target audience. The provision of a biosecurity code which is all encompassing should help.

3.5.4   The Government recognises that good biosecurity should form part of the education of livestock keepers and others associated with animals. The Government will ensure that biosecurity training is addressed in the programme taking forward the commitment announced on 26 March 2002 to review the effectiveness of training and education for farmers and other land managers.

3.5.5   Good biosecurity inevitably has a cost for farm businesses. However, it is a good investment. The Government needs to keep the possibility of providing financial incentives for good practice under review, and incorporate it where possible into Government policies. Possible examples of incentives for achievement of biosecurity standards might include abatement of levy payments or top up payments of subsidies under the reformed Common Agricultural Policy.

3.5.6   There may be scope for improving biosecurity by adapting and extending biosecurity standards in farm assurance schemes. As assurance schemes are privately run voluntary initiatives the scheme administrators would have to take this forward. The Government has written to them to draw their attention to the recommendations on assurance in the Lessons Learned Inquiry and to seek information on the extent to which biosecurity is already a condition of assurance schemes.

SECTION 4: EMERGENCY RESPONSE AND DISEASE CONTROL IN AN OUTBREAK

4.1 Planned approach

4.1.1   The Government's objective in tackling any fresh outbreaks of FMD will be to eradicate the disease as quickly as possible and to maintain the UK's disease-free status, as recommended by the inquiries. In doing so, the Government will seek to select a control strategy which:

- minimises the number of animals which need to be slaughtered, either to control the disease or on welfare grounds, and which keeps animal welfare problems to a minimum;

- causes the least possible disruption to the food, farming and tourism industries, to visitors to the countryside, and to rural communities and the wider economy;

- minimises damage to the environment and protects public health; and

- minimises the burden on taxpayers and the public at large.

4.1.2   The Government will base its decisions on the best available scientific and veterinary advice, including advice from the Defra Science Advisory Group, taking the views and interests of all stakeholders into account.

4.1.3   This section describes how the Government would approach an outbreak of FMD (or another animal disease). In many cases a considerable programme of work is required before all the elements become fully established parts of a response to a disease outbreak. In addition, the Government and in particular Defra will be working with stakeholders to produce an outcome which commands widespread acceptance. The circumstances of each outbreak are unique. The plans described below have to be read with this in mind.

4.2 Emergency response structures

4.2.1   The Government is committed to improving its emergency preparedness for an outbreak of exotic animal disease. Defra will lead in dealing with such an emergency, working closely with the Devolved Administrations and the local authorities. It has established an Emergency Preparedness Programme Board to ensure that full preparedness is achieved. This is chaired by the Director of the State Veterinary Service and includes representatives from other parts of Defra, the Devolved Administrations, the Environment Agency, the Local Government Association and the Local Authority Co-ordinators of Regulatory Services (LACORS).

4.2.2   The goals of the Emergency Preparedness Programme are to enable Defra and the Government to manage down risks, impacts and costs during a disease outbreak, to be ready at all times to take timely action to achieve this and, in addition, to reduce the probability of an outbreak. The Programme will drive forward work on policy issues, emergency operational issues and contingency plans. The work ranges from developing contingency plans for all exotic diseases, training staff in their use and exercising and testing them, through the development of new IT systems for recording data on animal disease control to work to control the illegal importation of meat and meat products into the UK and the development of vaccination and culling policies. A diagram of the programme plan is opposite.

Animal Disease Emergency Preparedness Programme Plan

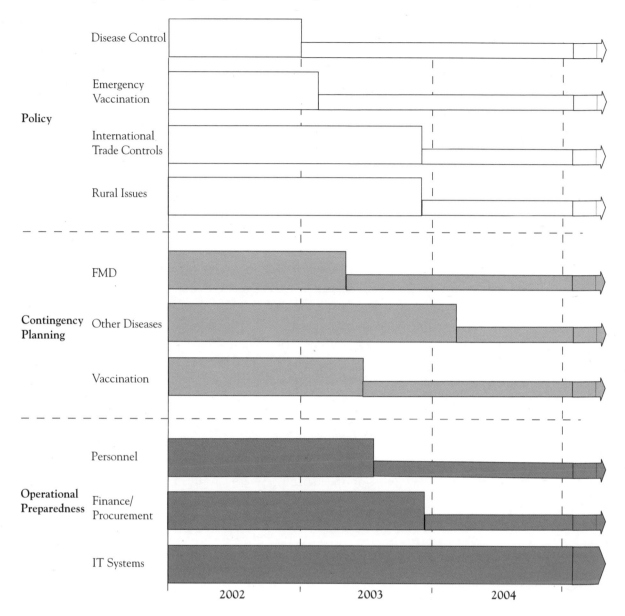

The Preparedness Programme

4.2.3   The Emergency Preparedness Programme Board is responsible for ensuring that all elements of the policies relating to the control of an outbreak of exotic animal disease such as handling suspect cases, decisions on culling policies, the approach to be taken on vaccination and policies relating to movement restrictions are up to date within the legal framework and in the light of other policy changes. The Board will check that operational readiness is being achieved by, for example, reviewing and developing the hierarchy of disposal options and the necessary related transport arrangements. The Board will ensure that where final policy decisions will not be possible until the nature of a disease outbreak is known, approaches are considered and a decision tree developed so that the factors involved and the process of decision making are transparent and open. The Government will also publish a protocol explaining how it will handle suspect cases of FMD and other vesicular diseases, and it will incorporate this too into the Contingency Plan.

4.2.4   Defra is developing organisations and structures which it would activate in a disease outbreak. These will provide the framework for the rapid establishment of the offices necessary to support the State Veterinary Service in controlling disease both across the country and in London. This will include the

National Disease Control Centre and local disease control centres based on existing animal health offices which will include teams to deal with finance, procurement and contracts and personnel as well as veterinary, technical and administrative staff engaged directly on disease control. Named and trained senior staff will head the offices and will be posted in as soon as a case is confirmed. The teams will have detailed guidance on their responsibilities and duties together with process maps and instructions to ensure that the offices run efficiently from the outset. Protocols for increasing numbers of staff by loans from other Departments are being developed. These arrangements strengthen those that existed at the beginning of the outbreak last year. In the longer term consideration will be given to more active engagement with all the emergency services in developing local centres.

4.2.5   Centrally, the national disease control centre will provide the means of directing and managing the disease control operation. It will also be the forum which provides a co-ordinated approach across Government Departments and brings in other operational partners such as the local authorities, police and those affected by the disease.

4.2.6   These structures not only provide the management structures for the operation but also the framework for strategic policy decisions and the tactical management of operations. They form an agreed basis for bringing in interested parties, the armed forces, and advice from the Defra Science Advisory Group that were not in place at the start of the outbreak in 2001. They reflect the developments that took place during the outbreak and the experience of staff who were involved. By agreeing and setting out these structures as part of the planning programme and by testing them in contingency exercises Defra can implement them rapidly and effectively when needed.

Staffing

4.2.7   The Cabinet Office is developing a protocol to manage the increase of staff numbers through the release by all Departments and Agencies of staff for any Department or Agency dealing with a major incident or civil emergency. The Civil Contingencies Secretariat is also reviewing the training and development available for senior managers across Whitehall to establish the skills necessary for managing emergencies. These measures will provide a flexible response to a range of possible challenges.

4.2.8   To replace and improve upon the current temporary arrangements, Defra is planning an emergency register listing competences and skills for staff willing to serve in an emergency. Contact records of staff who worked on FMD in 2001 in local offices and in headquarters have been retained.

4.2.9   Emergency preparedness requires all the systems, data recording and type of management information that will be required to be fully thought through, so that from the start of an outbreak the right systems can be implemented and information recorded. Lessons learned in 2001, when data handling, and information gathering was necessarily of a lower priority to controlling disease, are feeding into reviews of IT systems, and into the construction of the data recording and information management structures.

Management and direction

4.2.10   The inquiries have made recommendations on the importance of clear command lines and communication structures. The management structures that would be introduced in an emergency are being introduced as indicated above. They build on the reorganisation of the State Veterinary Service and its inclusion within the Operations and Service Delivery Directorate General in Defra and provide short clear lines of command, good liaison and better relationships.

4.2.11   One line of command will manage the disease control operation, from the Director of the State Veterinary Service, who will be Director of Operations, to Regional Operations Directors (RODs) who will lead and manage both the veterinary and administrative teams in the local Disease Control Centres.

The Director of Operations will, where possible, devolve operational decisions to the RODs, with guidance provided on when they should implement central operational policy and where veterinary judgement may be used. This approach builds on lessons learned in 2001 when there was some confusion over lines of command, the complexity of the arrangements was seen to hinder effective communication and the responsibilities at different levels were not always clear. The following diagram sets out the management structure within Defra, indicating the separation of strategy and operations. It also includes a proposed Government FMD Co-ordination Committee. This will provide the forum for reviewing strategies in wider Government context and for dealing with operational issues that affect other departments. This builds on the role that the Cabinet Office Briefing Room (COBR) took during the last outbreak. These structures are included in the contingency plans and their effectiveness will be tested when the plans are used in exercises. The Emergency Preparedness Programme Board will be concerned to ensure that these structures are understood and can be effectively implemented.

Single-Line Command Structure for Control of FMD

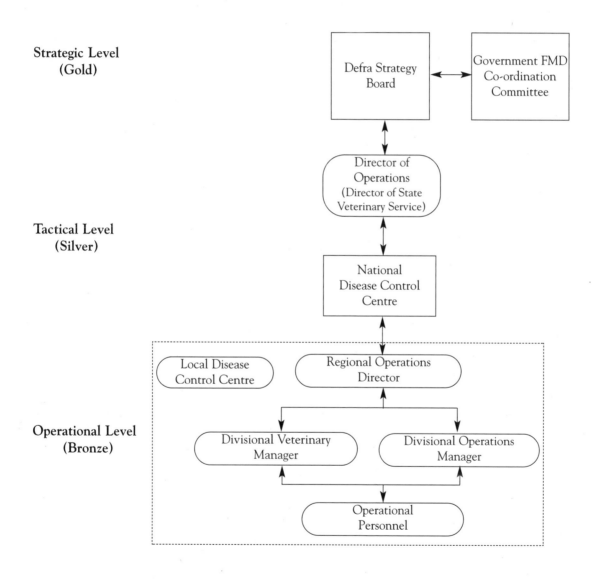

4.2.12   Defra is advertising across Government departments to recruit senior key personnel who will, in a disease emergency, move to fill senior posts as Regional Operations Directors leading the operation in the field, freeing divisional veterinary staff to apply their professional skills and judgement, and ensuring good communication and engagement with local stakeholders. Other named administrative staff will support them, who will also be posted in as soon as the disease is confirmed. They will lead the whole team in the local disease control centre and report to HQ on that basis. They will be responsible for managing an efficient office to provide administrative support to the veterinary operation and, if appropriate, for liaison with the Armed Forces. To prepare for an outbreak they will be trained in emergency management and dealing with the media and will be involved in exercises on the contingency plans to ensure they are familiar with their area and office. Defra will charge them to arrive at their post within a day or so of confirmation of an outbreak and ensure that the field operation and supporting administrative teams run efficiently from the very beginning of an outbreak.

4.2.13   The Welsh Assembly Government's interim contingency plan includes named individuals to populate operational structures in the event of any future crisis.

Engaging the Armed Forces

4.2.14   Defra will alert the Armed Forces immediately a case of FMD is confirmed so that they can offer advice and support to define their possible role. This will focus, in particular, on the rapid build up of logistical capability. One of the prime purposes of developing detailed contingency plans and the achievement of a state of emergency preparedness, which meets the objectives of the Programme Board, is to enable the operation to be immediately effective and so reduce the need for military involvement. Final decisions on the level and nature of the involvement of the Armed Forces would of course depend on other commitments at the time.

Additional staff

4.2.15   In addition to identifying key senior staff for local offices as a contingency, arrangements are in hand to post procurement and contracts experts into local disease control centres at the beginning of an outbreak and to build up finance teams from day one. To support these work areas, information and guidance would be available on the internal website to supplement the guidance that has long been available on veterinary and disease control matters. Defra would also draft in one or more personnel experts immediately and engage local staff from the Government News Network. The whole operation would be geared to ensure effective disease control within a framework of good local liaison and communication flow and an efficient administrative back up.

4.2.16   Defra would increase veterinary staff numbers immediately an outbreak was confirmed, depending on the national and local requirements of the Disease Control Centres. It would achieve this by drawing on other parts of the State Veterinary Service, and Defra agencies, and then as necessary from local veterinary practices, the Food Standards Agency, the Meat Hygiene Service and other Government departments, other areas of employment within the UK, internationally agreed protocols for vets from other countries, and recruitment of temporary veterinary staff. Following their valuable contribution in 2001, Defra would also seek assistance from veterinary colleges for veterinary students to assist and support the vets in specific areas, such as blood sampling and possible vaccination.

Organisation and systems

4.2.17   The experience gained last year by staff is being harnessed through workshops and through business process mapping to develop the most effective administrative systems for dealing with future outbreaks of disease. Increasingly these are IT based and provide the most efficient means of maintaining and developing systems that staff in offices across the country and in the field can use.

Scenario planning

4.2.18   Various strands of emergency preparedness will be brought together in developing scenarios for FMD contingencies. These will cover a range of possible outbreaks from one case to many simultaneously and will help to develop an assessment of the demands that the Government will need to meet in terms of, for example, personnel resources, disposal facilities, vaccination operations and cleansing and disinfection. They will also help to identify the resources needed by local authorities to enforce movement restrictions and ensure that the biosecurity requirements of Blue Boxes are understood and enforced. Their development is still at an early stage within Defra, but the Department will take it further with the assistance of stakeholders and operational partners to provide an agreed basis for action.

4.2.19   One of the most important elements of planning to control an outbreak is the involvement of local authorities because of their responsibility for enforcement and their role in other aspects of life which are affected both by the disease and the control operation. It will be very important to liaise with them over methods of carcass transport and disposal, over the impact of disposal, and over the management of movement restrictions for vehicles and pedestrians, and to engage the support of local organisations in helping those worst affected. Working on contingency planning exercises with local authority staff in seminars at the Emergency Planning College at Easingwold is one way in which staff in Defra are taking forward this element of preparedness.

Communications and media handling

4.2.20   The current Contingency Plan formalises a detailed timetable for the events which would trigger announcements to the media in a possible future outbreak. Defra alerts the media when 8 km livestock movement restrictions are imposed. A protocol ensures that all internal and stakeholder contacts are informed quickly. Defra will of course report confirmatory laboratory test results as soon as they are known. This largely captures the arrangements followed in 2001.

4.2.21   If an outbreak occurs, Defra will immediately and rapidly augment existing round-the-clock communications resources at HQ and regionally. To do this immediately, staff from other desks would drop other work, and the majority of the office would work exclusively on the outbreak. The Government will bring in extra staff rapidly and in future a more co-ordinated approach from the centre will assist Defra in this.

Cross-Government media handling

4.2.22   The Government Information and Communication Service central News Co-ordination Centre (NCC) is now well established. It has a range of capabilities - including call-off contracts - which it can adapt to different situations. It can augment a department's individual capacity or augment and co-ordinate the Government's effort as a whole.

4.2.23   A key issue is when to trigger NCC involvement. Normally, this will happen in any cross-Government crisis involving more than two departments. Then, NCC will take the lead in co-ordinating the public information effort and disseminating information within Government and key stakeholders. Where the situation is particularly fluid and fast moving, this will include a central press office.

4.2.24   Where the crisis is not on this scale, the NCC will work to support the communication effort of the lead department. Therefore in any future crisis, Defra would work closely with the NCC. It will either provide co-ordination, with the NCC disseminating information more widely to the Government News Network in the regions and others; or play a key role in delivering all departmental information and supporting the NCC's central lead.

HQ 'hub'

4.2.25   In forthcoming trial exercises Defra plans to set up a 'hub and spoke' system of information exchange with a central hub at HQ and communications "cells" in the regions. If successful this would form the backbone of all communications between the regions and the centre in the event of any crisis. Such a system would emphasise the importance of good communications and of maintaining the flow from the centre of guidance on policies, operational strategies and advice and from the flow from the cells of information on operations and local impacts.

4.2.26 A central Defra Briefing Unit, set up during the 2001 outbreak, collates and generates departmental briefing for use by the whole of Defra and the rest of Whitehall. Staff from this unit, along with other communication specialists would form the nucleus of a new multi-disciplinary "Communications Hub", co-located with the National Disease Control Centre and would be reinforced as soon as possible with veterinary expertise and others as appropriate. A specialist "webmaster" would take immediate steps to set up a crisis website. The Hub would make briefing available throughout Government by the use of the electronic cross-departmental briefing system known as the Knowledge Network. This system can be easily and rapidly updated.

Regional communications "cells"

4.2.27 Defra's London-based regional press desk (set up during the 2001 outbreak) now has a permanent role in Defra's communications strategy. It monitors regional media and works proactively with the Government News Network (GNN) to co-ordinate Defra output and coverage. It will ensure that regional links are established quickly.

4.2.28 One of Defra's first steps, as in 2001, would be to alert GNN to the need for additional resources. GNN would move staff to work within the regional Defra Disease Control Centres as in 2001 and Defra would reinforce at a local level to create regional communications "cells" capable of handling all operational, policy and media communications. Regional cells would ensure that stakeholders, front line staff and the local media were kept fully informed. They would also be the main information source for technical helplines if set up in affected areas. The cells would also feed back to the central hub details of local activity and intelligence, taking a role in local stakeholder meetings and co-ordinating briefing information.

4.2.29 Information would travel between the HQ 'hub' and regional communications centres by a variety of means, including Defra's Knowledge Network and the departmental intranet.

Wider regional communications

4.2.30 In a crisis there is a key need for enhanced communication at a regional level. This will involve Defra's many regionally based organisations and other rural key players such as tourism boards, Regional Development Agencies and local authorities. In an animal disease emergency, the Regional Operations Directors will be responsible for liaising with other stakeholders, operational partners and the public so that they are all fully informed of and involved in the disease control effort.

4.2.31 To facilitate this process, Defra is developing proposals to create regular regional contact groups which bring together, for each region, all parts of the Department (and, possibly other departments) operating in that region. This will deliver better joined-up working on the ground, delivering an improved service by getting more complete feedback from customers and stakeholders, and feeding back operational concerns to improve policy making. Such contact groups were not in place during the 2001 outbreak.

Speed of communications

4.2.32 Defra is exploring new systems for getting information quickly out to the field, which would be especially useful in a crisis situation. One of the main difficulties is that many field staff come into the office only rarely and when they do, often do not have the time to fully catch up on recent developments.

4.2.33 Subject to successful trials, mass text messaging ("blasting") and a dial-in message service - Defra Direct, would communicate alerts to new information and operational changes directly to field staff . Defra Direct would be a simple dial-in recorded message hotline, recorded at a fixed time once a day to highlight the day's developments and any updates to operational instructions or veterinary policy.

Stakeholder meetings

4.2.34   At national level, Defra would hold stakeholder meetings regularly as before. It will include these in the overall communications systems so that front line staff and helplines are fully briefed. Defra has been evaluating its relationships with its diverse stakeholders. It will produce a stakeholder strategy and set up a central stakeholder database. This will help identify appropriate contacts quickly in any future crisis.

Helplines

4.2.35   Defra has reviewed its helplines to identify how to make it easier for the public and customers to contact the appropriate part of the Department. Defra aims to consolidate the way these operate with a view to setting up a single access number. This contact centre would give callers information directly or transfer them to specialists. Defra will develop plans to provide contingency resources to rapidly expand capacity in the event of a crisis.

4.3   Disease control strategies

4.3.1   Each disease outbreak is different. Each has to be tackled at speed and - inevitably - with imperfect information. It will therefore not be possible to prescribe in detail which strategy will be followed in advance of knowing the circumstances of a particular outbreak. This calls for a flexible approach, which recognises that different approaches may be needed in different geographical areas or to deal with different diseases or different species.

4.3.2   The Government agrees with the Royal Society that a range of possible disease controls should be explored and available, including the strategy of vaccination to live, and, so far as is practicable, decisions taken in advance of outbreaks as to the strategy to be preferred in particular circumstances.

Decision tree

4.3.3   Defra officials have been working on a 'decision tree' for FMD control which will set out the criteria by which choices would be made between different strategies, depending on a range of factors. Decisions would be dependent on having relevant information available. Factors include the:

- strain of disease and its infectivity;

- species involved and stocking density;

- types of farms and topography in the area(s) involved;

- seasonal factors, e.g. volume of animal movements; and,

- environmental/climatic conditions (e.g. airborne spread).

Alongside wider issues such as the:

- availability of human resources (veterinary, slaughtermen, etc);

- availability of physical resources (e.g. for carcass disposal or of vaccine stocks);

- legal framework, public opinion, stakeholder views; and,

- economic considerations, both for farming and for other sectors e.g. tourism.

4.3.4   The Government is consulting stakeholders about the available FMD control strategies and the 'decision tree' approach. The intention is to publish a document that would explain in advance the possible strategies to be adopted in a future outbreak, depending on the nature of the outbreak. The Government believes this will not only aid transparency, and help to build public support, but also help to speed up decision making in the event of a future outbreak by resolving as many issues as possible beforehand.

Outbreaks of FMD

4.3.5   FMD is, rightly, a much-feared disease. It is highly infectious, extremely painful in some species such as cattle and can lead to abortion or be fatal to young animals. For many years the approach of the international community has been to seek to eradicate the disease. The approach has led to trade restrictions in areas where the disease is present and to slaughter of infected animals and those exposed to infection in order to stem the disease's spread. Indeed, at an international conference sponsored jointly by the UK and Dutch Governments and the EU, this basic approach was re-endorsed by Chief Veterinarians and representatives from across the world.

4.3.6   The sheer scale and impact of the unprecedented FMD outbreak of 2001 mercilessly exposed the full potential impact and the limitations of such a policy. That stark reality has led to the complete reappraisal of the disease control options available and of their use.

4.3.7   The Royal Society takes the view that "rapid culling of infected premises and known dangerous contacts, combined with movement control and rapid diagnosis, will remain essential to controlling FMD and most other highly infectious diseases," but "in many cases this will not be sufficient guarantee that the outbreak does not develop into an epidemic." It also accepts that, although much work remains to be done on what the potential of vaccination might be, - "emergency vaccination should now be considered as part of the control strategy from the start of any outbreak of FMD". (Royal Society key finding 7.) The Government accepts this and the other central recommendations on disease control of the Lessons Learned and Royal Society inquiries.

4.3.8   The inquiries investigated the issues involved in employing emergency vaccination. Between them they highlighted a range of significant questions that would need to be addressed, particularly as regards vaccination to live, but concluded that once these were resolved, the option of emergency vaccination to live should be the preferred approach.

4.3.9   The Government accepts that if emergency vaccination is used it should be on the basis of vaccinate-to-live wherever possible. During 2001 vaccination was used in the Netherlands, but as a means of managing disposal. All vaccinated animals were slaughtered. Vaccination-to-live was very seriously considered by the British Government at various points in the outbreak.

4.3.10   As the inquiry reports recognise, there is still work to be done to make emergency vaccination-to-live a fully viable control option - on the testing, on logistics, and on the marketability of products from vaccinated animals. European Union legislation will be a determining factor in some of these areas.

4.3.11   The EU Council Directive on FMD, 85/511 as amended, requires slaughter of all susceptible animals on infected premises, and provides for culling of susceptible animals on epidemiologically linked holdings (known as dangerous contacts). This reflects the EU's policy of adopting "FMD free without vaccination" status for all Member States, and is provided for in Defra's current FMD Contingency Plan.

4.3.12   Beyond this basic strategy, which will apply in all cases, there is a range of additional options and strategies potentially available to meet the circumstances of a particular outbreak and the scientific and veterinary advice. These include:—

- emergency vaccination (either to live or to kill; within an area or in a ring around an area);

- culling of other livestock exposed to the disease (e.g. premises under virus plumes, contiguous premises); and,

- pre-emptive or 'firebreak' culling of animals not on infected premises nor dangerous contacts nor necessarily exposed to the disease, in order to prevent the wider spread of the disease outwith an area.

Emergency vaccination

4.3.13   The Royal Society accepts, as does the Government, the need for validation of tests to distinguish vaccinated from infected animals. The Government is aware of a variety of NSP (non-structural protein) tests that are at differing levels of validation. There are currently a number of research projects in the UK, Europe and America and many of the European groups are partners in a European Union Concerted Action project on FMD diagnosis. The main limiting factor for the validation of such tests is the availability of suitable panels of sera, especially from vaccinated and then challenged animals. Defra is supporting research into this area. In addition, the Government also accepts that there is a need to develop accepted strategies for surveillance after vaccination. Indeed, this is something that the OIE has under consideration.

4.3.14   Constraints on environmentally safe disposal methods, which would need the active involvement of the Environment Agency at the earliest possible stage, will be one of the factors in decisions on whether to adopt emergency vaccination, whether to live or to kill.

4.3.15   The acceptability and hence the saleability of products from vaccinated animals is a key issue. The apparent lack of support last year from the food and farming sectors was a key factor in the Government deciding not to vaccinate cattle in Cumbria and Devon. The Lessons Learned report highlights this issue.

4.3.16   The Government is completely satisfied that meat and meat products from vaccinated animals can enter the food chain. The Food Standards Agency advise that the health implications from eating meat, milk or other produce from animals that have been treated with authorised FMD vaccines are negligible. The Government is committed to tackling these issues, in consultation with all interested parties, so that it is in a position to trigger an emergency vaccination campaign should the need arise. This process of consultation will take some time to complete. In the meantime, the Government needs to retain its full armoury of weapons against the disease. Operational issues relating to emergency vaccination are in Annex III.

4.3.17   Emergency vaccination can only take place as the subject of EU decision. In order for a vaccination strategy to be fully effective there would need to be a concerted EU approach and a new legislative framework at EU level. The Government will actively pursue with the Commission the need for a new framework for the use of vaccination and for the research effort on FMD and animal disease across the EU.

4.3.18   Last year the EU Decision authorising use of emergency vaccination in the UK laid down a number of post-vaccination controls. It is possible that the new draft FMD Directive will include similar provisions. If so, these would require meat from vaccinated animals to be heat treated until at least 30 days have elapsed following vaccination and further restrictions for a period of 12 months. Meat would have to be de-boned and matured. There are known to be problems in achieving the required maturation (to get the meat down to the required pH level) in pork and lamb, which is why countries which vaccinate tend to only export beef. The taking of semen, ova and embryos from vaccinated animals would also be prohibited. Vaccinated animals would not be permitted to move out of the vaccination zone for 12 months (except under licence to slaughter).

4.3.19   The FMD status of all countries is ultimately determined by the OIE. Should emergency vaccination be used, it would be necessary to satisfy all concerned that FMD virus has been eradicated, that all controls relevant to vaccination had been followed, and that vaccinated animals did not harbour FMD. So the Government will also develop with stakeholders an exit strategy designed to permit an early return to 'disease-free without vaccination' status for the UK.

4.3.20   The Royal Society recommends that Defra should explore with the EU and OIE what improvements to vaccines and surveillance tests are required to allow restoration of disease free status to be based entirely on surveillance results without the requirement for a minimum waiting period. Changes to the OIE code in May 2002 reduced the minimum waiting period from 12 to 6 months following emergency vaccination, provided a stamping out policy had been deployed and a serological survey had adequately demonstrated the absence of infection. The Government believes that this will allow emergency vaccination to be more readily used as a disease control strategy in the future.

4.3.21   The UK is an importing country as well as an exporting country. The Government therefore is unable to agree that a minimum waiting period following an outbreak should be entirely abolished. Such conditions are intended to protect importing countries - including the UK itself - from FMD.

Routine (prophylactic) vaccination

4.3.22   The inquiry reports acknowledge that because of the EU's declared policy of stamping out the disease and maintaining its "FMD free without vaccination" status, existing EU law only provides for the use of vaccination in an emergency and then only as an aid to disease control.

4.3.23   The Royal Society proposes that the Government should take the lead in developing an international research programme aimed at an improved vaccine that would permit routine and global vaccination of livestock against FMD and other diseases of animals on List A maintained by the OIE. The Royal Society report underlines the complications associated with routine vaccination - including the variety of FMD strains and serotypes, the short immunity period conferred by current vaccines, the need for all susceptible animals to be vaccinated, and the severe trade restrictions that would be imposed.

4.3.24   The Government agrees that an improved vaccine that would permit routine and global vaccination of livestock against all strains of FMD is a desirable long-term goal. This is an issue of international rather than national scope and would be most effectively led by an international organisation such as the FAO or possibly as an EU initiative. The Government intends to raise this issue with its EU partners in discussions on future research priorities.

Pre-emptive culling

4.3.25   The culling of animals that have been exposed to the disease is provided for under existing domestic legislation. The Lessons Learned Inquiry recommended that provision should be made for the possible application of pre-emptive culling policies, if justified by well-informed veterinary and scientific advice, and judged to be appropriate to the circumstances. The Government agrees, and powers for pre-emptive (or preventive) culling of animals not exposed to FMD infection in order to get ahead of the disease and stop it spreading are proposed in the Government's Animal Health Bill. The Government has published for consultation a draft Disease Control (Slaughter) Protocol to explain the circumstances in which different culling strategies may be used.

4.3.26   Although such an approach was not needed in 2001 (except insofar as it was part of the effect of the Dutch Government's vaccinate and cull policy), there were moments of great danger during that outbreak when a shift in the pattern of the disease might have been catastrophic. The Government thus believes, as did the Lessons Learned Inquiry, that it is necessary at present to maintain such flexibility.

4.4   Movement restrictions

4.4.1   Movement controls in the absence of disease were discussed in Section 3.3. On suspicion of disease, the Royal Society recommends that the Government should impose a local movement ban while samples are sent to an OIE reference laboratory for diagnosis. The EU requires that an approved national laboratory carries the diagnosis of FMD. In the case of the UK, this is the Institute for Animal Health at

Pirbright, which is one of four OIE – approved laboratories and the Food and Agriculture Organisation World Reference Laboratory. The imposition of movement bans in an 8km radius around the suspect case is part of current practice and was applied promptly in February 2001. It has been successfully applied in four suspect cases since FMD was eradicated, all of which turned out negative, and is part of Defra's Contingency Plan.

4.4.2   Both the Royal Society and Lessons Learned Inquiry reports favour an immediate national ban on livestock movements once the first case is confirmed. The Government would maintain this until it determined the extent of the outbreak when it would review it. There would be clear instructions on how to deal with animals in transit at the time the ban is imposed. The Government agrees that, in any future outbreak, once a case has been confirmed it should put in place a national ban on the movement of susceptible livestock – along with a suspension of livestock markets at once while tracings continue. Defra's Contingency Plan for FMD sets this policy out.

4.4.3   The Government will aim to allow livestock movements to resume as quickly as possible after a national ban has been imposed. This will help to minimise animal welfare difficulties and to maintain supplies to the food chain. This will be easiest outside infected areas once these have been established and the potential spread of the disease ascertained. Arrangements will also be made to facilitate such movements within infected areas where this can be done without raising undue risks of disease spread. The aim will be to lift additional movement restrictions imposed as a result of the outbreak as quickly as possible. The period and measures would depend on the scale, geographical extent and duration of any outbreak.

Public rights of way

4.4.4   The Government recognises that empowering local authorities to close footpaths and other public rights of way outside Infected Areas at the start of the 2001 outbreak, although undertaken for the best of motives and – initially at least – widely supported, went too far. The Royal Society report (at paragraph 3.24) points out that the actual risk of walkers who come into contact with livestock spreading the disease is poorly understood. The veterinary risk assessments carried out by MAFF and later by Defra suggest that the risk is very low, unless there is direct contact with successive groups of livestock.

4.4.5   Accordingly, the Contingency Plan makes clear that, in the event of a future FMD outbreak, public rights of way closures would be restricted to the Infected Areas and, if circumstances were similar to those of 2001, would probably be required only in a 3km radius around infected premises. The Government plans to produce a protocol on public rights of way closures to help guide local authorities, major landowners such as the National Trust, and members of the public. A draft is being issued for consultation.

4.5   Biosecurity during an outbreak

4.5.1   The Royal Society recommends that when an outbreak occurs, the Government should instigate enhanced biosecurity at all levels, and that it should offer advice and support to help farmers and others achieve this. It had in mind a 72 hours total ban on movements on or off farms in a 10km radius surrounding the infected premises. The Lessons Learned Inquiry recommended that the Government should build the use of Restricted Infected Areas ("Blue Box") biosecurity arrangements into contingency plans. The "Blue Box" controls in 2001 involved additional licensing, inspection and enforcement efforts by local authorities on vehicles entering farms in the designated areas. The controls were resource intensive but provided better compliance with biosecurity requirements.

4.5.2   The Government accepts the thrust of these recommendations. As a first step, the FMD Contingency Plan provides that, in the event of a fresh outbreak, the Government will impose a Restricted Infected Area, rather than the normal Infected Area, in a 10km radius.

4.6   Disposal

4.6.1   The Lessons Learned Inquiry has recommended that the burning of animals on mass pyres should not be used again as a strategy for disposal of slaughtered animals. The Government has reviewed its disposal strategy for future animal disease outbreaks in the light of the experience of the 2001 epidemic, its studies of disposal costs, and the recommendations of the inquiries.

4.6.2   A revised disposal hierarchy is set out in the FMD Contingency Plan, as follows:

Commercial incineration

Rendering

Licensed landfill

4.6.3   This has altered significantly from the hierarchy agreed in April 2001 with the Environment Agency and the Department of Health. The level and availability of disposal capacity using these routes will be a factor in considering the possible use of alternatives to wider culling strategies, for example emergency vaccination. The Government will not use mass pyres in the future but it cannot completely rule out the use of alternative disposal routes such as on-farm or mass burial if demand exceeds the capacity of the preferred options of incineration/rendering and licensed landfill. In planning disposal methods Defra will liaise with the local authorities to develop transport routes and disposal options that pose least risk to the local community and environment. One consequence of the new approach is that the mass burial sites acquired by the Government during the 2001 epidemic can now be disposed of, although the Government will continue to take responsibility for monitoring and managing the areas which hold carcasses.

Incineration

4.6.4   Although rendering was the most favoured option for disposal during the FMD outbreak of 2001 (mainly due to the much larger capacity these plants could offer in comparison to incineration) incineration is now placed at the top of the hierarchy. This is because a review of capacity found that large animal incineration would be able to cope with the first 48-72 hours of a new outbreak. Defra will put contingency contracts in place with incinerator plant operators to confirm these arrangements.

4.6.5   Suitable rendering plants are currently contracted to either dispose of animal by-products or bovine carcasses under the Over Thirty Months scheme. To remove a rendering plant from its normal operation, transfer it across to FMD material and then subsequently thoroughly cleanse and disinfect the plant is a lengthy and costly process. Therefore disposal through incineration will remain the first option in the first 48-72 hours of a new outbreak. If it becomes evident that incineration capacity is not going to be able to cope with demand then the Government would rapidly call upon rendering plants.

4.6.6   Seven incinerator operators have agreed to take carcasses if required, although one could only be used if it fell inside an infected area (as there are susceptible livestock nearby).

Rendering

4.6.7   Defra currently has a call-off agreement in place with a rendering plant to provide rendering capacity at 48 hours notice. Similar arrangements are in place in Scotland. These arrangements were not in place in 2001; instead Defra relied on the existing contracts held by the Rural Payments Agency. If demand exceeds this, it will bring further plants on stream. There are some 20 rendering plants in the UK but only 7 or 8 are likely to be suitable given their size or location. Defra would also seek to minimise the distances that carcasses were transported when bringing plants on-line. Defra has established a number of disease scenarios and using a range of modelling techniques it will develop a series of model outbreaks. It will then apply the disposal options to those models and identify key trigger points. This work will build on the experience of last year and the contracts the Rural Payments Agency already have in place with rendering operators.

4.6.8   Defra will work closely with the rendering industry to ensure that best use can be made of existing capacity.

Licensed landfill

4.6.9   Licensed landfill would be used if demand exceeds capacity at incineration and rendering plants. Defra is working to agree how licensed landfill capacity could be used, taking into account proximity to areas of the country with a high livestock density. Defra is leading discussions with representatives of the landfill industry to identify the most suitable sites.

Development of the future disposal hierarchy

4.6.10   The Government recognises that there are a number of factors that may impact on the disposal hierarchy in the future. These include the implementation of possible new environmental or waste management legislation and any changes to capacity and accessibility of all the disposal outlets. Defra will review the hierarchy regularly, in consultation with relevant stakeholders, to take account of these issues.

4.7   Welfare

4.7.1   Concern for animal welfare is at the heart of contingency planning for any future disease outbreak or emergency. In the case of a disease outbreak or emergency where the animals are killed, the plan will include the already well established procedures to maintain welfare standards during emergency slaughter. The assessment will also include the wider welfare impact of culling. For example, culling can have a welfare benefit if it shortens the time course of the outbreak and thereby reduces the needs for long-term movement restrictions. There are also welfare aspects to the vaccination option. While a "vaccinate to live" strategy could mean that fewer animals need to be culled there is a welfare cost in that vaccination also involves movement restrictions. Defra will take all of this into account in welfare planning.

4.7.2   Where possible, animals should be kept alive and healthy where they are. This is first of all the responsibility of the farmer, but there may be need for Government assistance through a licensed movement scheme or an arrangement to move fodder to animals precluded from movements. An animal welfare disposal scheme is an option of very last resort, as it is clearly undesirable to slaughter animals unless absolutely necessary. The Government would not offer compensation; experience has shown that payments to farmers under such schemes can provide a disincentive for them to take responsibility for looking after their animals, and may also create a false market. Nevertheless, such schemes must remain part of the contingency planning process. Defra will continue to work on the amount of detailed contingency planning needed adequately to protect animal welfare. The key indicator for welfare schemes will be the number of welfare problems resolved.

4.8 Compensation

4.8.1   The Lessons Learned Inquiry and the National Audit Office report revealed serious problems in the system of compensation for slaughtered livestock operated through the 2001 epidemic – the greatest single cost to the taxpayer, amounting to £1.2 billion. The Government believes that fundamental changes are needed here both in the principles involved and the administration. The Government is currently reviewing the arrangements for compensation payments. It is also working on policy options for risk sharing of costs in dealing with future animal disease outbreaks with the livestock industry. One possibility under consideration is a levy; the Government would only implement this following the establishment of a definitive movements regime and further progress on illegal imports, and it would set the level taking full account of farm incomes.

4.8.2   The Animal Health Act 1981 requires the payment of compensation at the value of the animal immediately before the time it was affected with FMD or, for animals not showing clinical signs, the value at the time of slaughter. Similar, though not necessarily identical, arrangements apply for a number of other animal diseases. In most cases valuation is undertaken by a professional valuer prior to slaughter of the animals. During the 2001 outbreak, values for animals tended to rise as more and more were slaughtered. The Government's major priority in fighting FMD was to slaughter animals as soon as possible to curtail spread of the disease. With hindsight, the introduction of Standard Valuations – in an effort to speed up the valuation and slaughter process – was not successful. Livestock owners retained the option of having individual valuation and the majority did so. The absence of markets in effect withdrew a benchmark for the valuers and the Standard Valuations tended to set a floor on the market. In addition, many animals were slaughtered at a time in their life when they would not normally be slaughtered or sold – for example, at the peak of their production cycle. The Government is keen to address these issues in both the short and the longer term.

4.8.3   In the short term, as part of the process of tightening up procedures, Defra is moving to having a formal national list of valuers approved on the basis of their qualifications and experience in livestock valuation. The first valuers were approved in October and more will be approved in November. On appointment each valuer receives detailed instructions on carrying out valuations. The fees for valuation have been revised from the much criticised basis of 1% of valuation (with daily minima and maxima of £500 and £1500) used in 2001 to an hourly rate for time spent at the valuation and reasonable travelling time.

4.8.4   Secondly, Defra is appointing a panel of senior monitor valuers. It will be their role to review the instructions and guidance to valuers and agree additional ones needed during an outbreak. They will review valuations in disease outbreaks.

4.8.5   Thirdly, Defra is also currently undertaking a study of FMD 2001 valuations to determine if there were patterns or trends in factors affecting valuations. The study will be based on a sample of payment files and will collect and analyse supporting documentation to help explain the reasons for the valuations reached. The study should be able to report its findings by the end of the year. Defra will use this to compare with and provide explanations to observations made by EU Auditors and the National Audit Office, for example, regarding the high levels of valuations. It will also use it to inform discussions on reform of animal valuation policy.

4.8.6   In the slightly longer term, a review of all the animal disease compensation arrangements is also being undertaken with a view to longer-term rationalisation and simplification. Part of this process will be to look at the case for compulsory standard valuations that would apply for compensation for all notifiable animal diseases. This would remove the need for individual valuation in many or most cases.

Such a system would help speed up the slaughtering process and would ensure a greater degree of uniformity in animal valuation. Defra intends to consult on rationalised compensation proposals by the end of 2002. Compulsory standard valuations would facilitate estimates of the funds which would need to be raised from industry and would also sit well with standard levy rates. Rationalisation of compensation will require an overhaul of primary and secondary legislation. A complete rationalisation of compensation may not therefore be implemented before 2004.

4.8.7   The Lessons Learned Inquiry recommended that the joint Defra Industry Working Group for Animal Disease Insurance ensure that its scope and membership is set widely enough to address valuation and compensation issues highlighted by the 2001 outbreak. The Group has met three times to discuss both animal disease compensation and animal disease levy/insurance options, and Defra will advise it of the results of consultations described in this section.

ANNEX I: RESPONSE TO INDIVIDUAL RECOMMENDATIONS

Lessons Learned Recommendations

RECOMMENDATION	RESPONSE
LL R1 We recommend that the Government, led by Defra, should develop a national strategy for animal health and disease control positioned within the framework set out in the report of the Policy Commission on the Future of Farming and Food. This strategy should be developed in consultation and partnership with the farming industry and with representatives of the wider rural economy. The European Commission, the devolved administrations in Scotland and Wales, local authorities and other agencies of government should be involved In this process. (p12)	Accept. The Government is committed to preparing an Animal Health and Welfare Strategy, which has also been recommended by the Policy Commission and the Royal Society. These inquiries provide invaluable guidance on the areas on which the Strategy should concentrate. The Government will engage the widest possible interests in its preparation.
LL R2 We recommend that lessons learned be routinely reviewed in the light of changing circumstances. Policies, plans and preparations should be adapted accordingly. (p25)	Accept. The Government recognises the need to review lessons, policies and plans in the light of changing circumstances. In terms of contingency plans for animal diseases, the Government agrees that plans will have to be kept under constant review. Similar steps are being taken by the Welsh Assembly Government.
LL R3 We recommend that there be a reappraisal of Local Veterinary Inspectors' roles and conditions. (p28)	Accept. Defra is undertaking a review of the current use of private veterinary surgeons, inviting comment from the main stakeholders. Defra is seeking in particular to improve the training of Local Veterinary Inspectors and their use in emergency situations.
LL R4 We recommend that where regional boundaries of Government Offices do not match those of local authorities or other agencies of government, special provision should be made in contingency planning for management and communications during a crisis.	Accept. The Government fully appreciates the efficiency gains from having common regional boundaries. Where this is not the position liaison with all operational agencies particularly across boundaries is emphasised as an important part of local contingency planning. In addition, the Civil Contingencies Secretariat provides the central focus for the cross-departmental and cross-agency co-ordination necessary for the UK to deal effectively with the domestic impact of disruptive challenges and crises. There are also plans to establish dedicated contingency planning teams in each Government Office region.

RECOMMENDATION	RESPONSE
LL R5 We recommend that the Government build an up to date database of livestock, farming and marketing practices. This should include research to examine the evolution of regional livestock stocking densities and implications for disease risk control. (p30)	<u>Not accepted in this form.</u> The Government recognises the importance of being well informed on farming practices and on the location and numbers of livestock. A major programme of work is in hand to improve livestock identification and tracing and this will, in due course, enable comprehensive databases on livestock holdings. At the same time, Defra has an active programme of stakeholder engagement, designed to ensure that officials are up-to-date with changes in practice, and have strong links with the industry. In view of the rapid pace of change in farming practices, especially in the light of planned changes to the subsidy regimes, the Government does not believe it would be practicable or cost-effective to develop a separate database of farming practices. The Animal Health and Welfare Strategy will consider the links between animal health and animal husbandry.
LL R6 We recommend that contingency plans set out procedures to be followed in the event that an emergency expands beyond worst-case expectations. (p36)	<u>Accept.</u> Scenario planning is under way to provide the background for many aspects of disease control including vaccination and disposal. Defra is developing its arrangements through cross-departmental exercises and work with the Civil Contingencies Secretariat to increase its staff resources. The Welsh Assembly Government is also involved in these exercises.
LL R7 We recommend that provision be made in contingency plans for rapid prioritisation of a Department's work in the face of a crisis, and for speedy reassignment of resources. (p36)	<u>Accept.</u> Proposals are currently being drawn up to ensure that Defra and other Departments, in response to an initiative from the Civil Contingencies Secretariat, can respond quickly in emergency situations, provide staff both within Defra and to other Government Departments and put in place arrangements for mobilising help from other Departments. In Defra the Management Board will consider how work should be prioritised in the event of a crisis and how resources should be reassigned, taking into account the possible nature, location and duration of such an event.

RECOMMENDATION	RESPONSE
<u>LL R8</u> We recommend that Defra develop its human resources plans for use in emergency. In particular they should focus on how staff numbers and expertise can be rapidly increased at a time of crisis. This should be developed in England in consultation with the Cabinet Office, the regional Co-ordination unit and the network of Government Offices. Similar arrangements should be developed in Scotland and Wales. (p36)	<u>Accept.</u> The Cabinet Office is developing a protocol for managing the release by all Departments of staff for any Department dealing with a major incident or civil contingency. This is being developed as a Memorandum of Understanding.

The Civil Contingencies Secretariat will also develop managers with skills suitable for managing emergencies, drawn from across Whitehall, who will be able to provide support either for their own Department or for others.

These measures are designed to provide a flexible response to a range of possible challenges, rather than specifically an outbreak of animal disease. They will complement and support the contingency plans developed by each Department and Agency for those areas of public service for which they are responsible. The Regional Co-ordination Unit/Government Office network is fully involved in the development of these measures.

Defra is seeking to identify people within Government service who have the necessary skills and who would be willing to fill key posts in an animal disease emergency and those who would be available for wider administrative tasks. This will implement that part of the National Audit Office recommendation 3, which calls for contingency plans to include the deployment of staff.

Similarly, the Welsh Assembly Government is actively working on plans to release trained human resources for use in an emergency. This is covered in their Contingency Plan. |
| <u>LL R9</u> We recommend that accepted best practice in risk analysis be used by Defra and others in developing livestock health and disease control strategies. (p38) | <u>Accept.</u> Defra is using formal risk assessment techniques on illegal imports and many aspects of work on Transmissible Spongiform Encephalopathies. The same approach is also being applied to animal movement controls. The Contingency Plan will also be based on risk analysis as recommended by the National Audit Office recommendation 1. |

RECOMMENDATION	RESPONSE
LL R10 We recommend that Government departments ensure that their own internal departmental arrangements properly resource contingency planning work. This should be monitored by the National Audit Office. (p39)	Accept. As a condition of the SR2002 settlement, Departments are required to agree with the Civil Contingencies Secretariat (CCS) their contribution to building the agreed capabilities, detailing what measures they propose to deliver, the timescale and the associated resources. Departments, the CCS and the Treasury will work together to ensure that these plans are in place. The CCS will consult the National Audit Office to consider their role in the monitoring process.
LL R11 We recommend that the Government publish a biennial report to the nation on the level of preparedness to tackle animal disease emergencies. The first report should be published in 2003 and include measures of achievement against goals. (p39)	Accept in principle. Defra accepts the principle of giving a regular account of the level of preparedness to tackle animal disease emergencies, though the precise mechanism and ownership needs to be considered further. The views of stakeholders will be taken during the consultation on the Animal Health and Welfare Strategy.
LL R12 We recommend that the Government ensure that best practice from import regimes elsewhere be incorporated with domestic practices where appropriate. (p47)	Accept in principle. The Government agrees on the need to learn from others' experience where applicable, but the results have to be applied to our own circumstances. Controls that work in relatively small international ports and airports with low throughput may not be practicable in Dover or Heathrow, where the majority of freight and passengers are travelling from within a free trade area.
LL R13 We recommend that the European Commission lead a targeted risk based approach designed to keep FMD out of EU Member States. The UK should work alongside other EU Member States to highlight areas of greater risk. (p47)	Accept in principle. This is primarily a matter for the European Commission. The Government will be discussing with them the findings from the Lessons Learned Inquiry. We will also share with them the results of the 'illegal imports' Risk Assessment. The global situation with regard to the occurrence of FMD and other diseases, particularly with regard to its third country trading partners, is monitored closely by both the European Commission and the UK either through direct contacts with third countries, via the Office International des Epizooties (OIE) or through the FAO European Commission on FMD.

RECOMMENDATION	RESPONSE
LL R14 We recommend that Defra be given responsibility for co-ordinating all the activities of Government to step up efforts to keep illegal meat imports out of the country. This should include better regulations and improved surveillance on illegal imports of meat and meat products. (p48)	<u>Further consideration.</u> A considerable programme of action on illegal imports is already under way, with Defra in the lead. Following a Cabinet Office study, all activity against smuggling of meat, animal products, fish and plant matter will be brought together in HM Customs & Excise and backed by a new dedicated target in Customs for service delivery in this area. There will be substantially improved co-ordination between the main control agencies, and between these agencies and Customs, under the oversight of a new ministerial group. The Government will also seek a step-change in the coordination and delivery of local authority inspection of imported foodstuffs and products of animal origin at ports within one year. Thereafter the Government will then look hard again at the case for bringing these functions from local authorities into a central agency, or delivering them from other routes.

Defra will re-examine the Action Plan later this year. |
| **LL R15** We recommend that the UK prohibition of swill feeding of catering waste containing meat products continue. The UK should continue to support a ban at EU level. (p49) | <u>Accept.</u> The Government fully supports the recommendation to continue the ban on swill feeding of catering waste containing meat products. The Government has also supported proposed EU legislation to introduce a Europe wide ban. Regulation (EC) No 1774/2002 of the European Parliament and of the Council of 3 October 2002 laying down health rules concerning animal by-products not intended for human consumption introduces a ban on swill feeding from 1 November 2002 for all Member States other than Germany and Austria, which have requested a transition period. |
| **LL R16** We recommend that in all suspected cases of FMD, the response reflect the experience of the emergency services, where speed and urgency of action govern decision-making. (p61) | <u>Accept.</u> By publishing its disease control protocols and its contingency plans, the Government intends to make known in advance of an outbreak as many as possible of the key factors to be considered during the emergency. In addition, the experience of dealing with the FMD outbreak in 2001 and ongoing contingency planning with those involved in the emergency services will contribute to ensuring that contingency plans are developed which will form the basis for rapid and effective decision making. |

RECOMMENDATION	RESPONSE
LL R17 We recommend that the State Veterinary Service consider forming a national network of 'flying squad' teams capable of responding to an alert. The continuing occurrence of false alarms can then be used constructively to maintain readiness and to practise routines. (p61)	Further consideration. Defra fully accepts the importance of ensuring that additional staff can be posted quickly to support work on a disease outbreak and is looking at ways of achieving this. Lessons will be learned from "false alarms" in developing the most effective system.

Key components of Disease Control Centres have already been identified including Regional Operations Directors, staff experienced in personnel, finance, contracts and procurements. The senior posts, to be held on a contingency basis, are now being advertised in all Government Departments. |
| **LL R18** We recommend that use be made of alternative sources of information and intelligence during crises. (p71) | Accept. The Government has reflected this recommendation in the FMD Contingency Plan. The Government fully appreciates the need to involve all stakeholders and will draw on a wide range of sources of information such as local authorities and other local organisations in developing intelligence during crises. |
| **LL R19** We recommend that Defra's Geographical Information System and the Integrated Administration and Control System (IACS) be designed so that they can be used more effectively for disease control purposes. (p72) | Accept in principle. There are a number of systems within Defra, each designed to deal with different aspects of business. Defra is currently developing a Geographical Information (GI) strategy which will cover the use of GI across core Defra, its agencies and selected Non-Departmental Public Bodies. The strategy will provide an overall corporate framework which business areas will use to determine how GI is used to support Defra objectives. This will ensure that GI data and application development activities that could have benefits to more than one business area are managed to deliver maximum benefits to Defra as a whole.

Data from the Integrated Administration and Control System (IACS) is used by the Rural Payments Agency (RPA) for Common Agricultural Policy subsidy payment and control purposes. In modernising its payment systems the RPA is developing a Rural Land Register (RLR) to support IACS in providing a key corporate data set.

This RLR component for IACS is due to be in place by 1 January 2004, but there is also the scope to extend the RLR to encompass all agricultural parcels not just those that are IACS |

RECOMMENDATION	RESPONSE

registered. Detailed plans on what other data should be captured have still to be developed and there are a number of issues concerning the confidentiality of IACS information and its disclosure. The RPA is working with the State Veterinary Service (SVS) and the GI strategy project board to take these initiatives forward.

The SVS is also developing a new Disease Control System which will have integrated GI components and be designed to use the RLR together with other key corporate datasets in any future disease outbreak. The new system is expected to be in place by the end of 2004. In Wales, a Geographical Information System for all IACS land in Wales will be completed by March 2003.

LL R20 We recommend that Defra lay out milestones for investment and achievement for improved management information systems. (p73)

Accept. Defra recognises that management information is an important part of both managing a disease outbreak and in providing Ministers and senior officials with the information to communicate effectively with both external and internal stakeholders and the general public. The State Veterinary Service project to develop a new Disease Control System is subject to the Office of Government Commerce's Gateway Review process, which sets clear milestones for development and requires that a Business Case hurdle be cleared before progressing.

LL R21 We recommend that data capture and management information systems be kept up to date and reflect the best practice.(p73)

Accept. Defra accepts that it is crucial that its systems are capable of capturing and analysing a large volume of data without delay. A current review (by external consultants) of IT systems in use in the State Veterinary Service (SVS) has just been completed and its findings will be considered urgently to ensure that the SVS's present and future systems not only reflect best practice but also support any necessary revisions to its business processes. The report of the Review Team suggests that its implementation will require that the SVS develop a service strategy to establish value added services to be provided to key customers, and that the IT systems should be developed around three core elements: a case management system, a farm diary and a data warehouse, with the latter supporting analysis of disease surveillance information to assist policy development. Early analysis suggests that implementation of the recommendations of the report would take 3 or 4 years to conclusion.

RECOMMENDATION	RESPONSE
LL R22 We recommend that the contingency plans of Defra, the Scottish Executive and the National Assembly for Wales specify the measures needed during an epidemic to monitor progress and report to key stakeholders. (p73)	Accept. Work is underway in the State Veterinary Service to review and improve the information systems used to capture data during normal work which can then be effectively and rapidly applied during a disease outbreak. The ways in which progress in controlling an outbreak of disease will be monitored will be agreed and reported to key stakeholders at the beginning of the outbreak.
LL R23 We recommend that standard definitions of all important parameters of information be agreed in advance. (p73)	Accept. Work has started on agreeing standard definitions for the data fields to support veterinary surveillance in a database that will be used in "peace time" to monitor and measure the level and distribution of disease. The need for standard definitions to be agreed in advance will also be a key factor in Defra's work to develop a new Disease Control System (see Lessons Learned recommendation 19 and Royal Society recommendation 6.1)
A key part of this is the data on the distribution of animals and a number of initiatives are under way to standardise definitions and rationalise current data sets in Defra. The Customer Registration Project (formerly the Single Business Identifier Project), will result in a single Defra wide agricultural business register integrated with a Geographic Information System (GIS) based Rural Land Register. The Rural Payments Agency and England Rural Development Plan Business Register will cover around 80% of Defra's customers over the next two years and Defra wishes to extend the work to cover all farms and businesses that have dealings with the Department so that these customers can use a single identifier.
This project will provide a more defined relationship between agricultural businesses and their geographical locations, and be invaluable in any future outbreaks. There is also a major requirement for a single business register in several parts of Defra in support of rural economies. For example, the Livestock Identification and Tracing Programme will use this register to improve the collection and maintenance of data regarding farm animals for disease control and monitoring purposes. The Programme proposes to develop a single centralised system holding all livestock information and linked to a GIS. It will address any data inconsistency issues and achieve major improvements in efficiency.

RECOMMENDATION	RESPONSE
LL R24 We recommend contingency plans at a regional level include mechanisms for making effective use of local voluntary resources. (p74)	<u>Accept.</u> Local contingency plans will include the requirement to make the best use of offers of voluntary assistance taking into account any aspects of health and safety requirements which may apply.
LL R25 We recommend that dedicated control systems be ready for use in a sustained emergency, and regularly tested as part of the contingency planning process. (p74)	<u>Accept.</u> Financial training and the availability of financial guidance, forms and advice online for staff in local offices are part of the planned approach to ensuring that financial control is managed efficiently from the very beginning of an outbreak. Electronic contract management will enhance visibility of the supply chain at the local, regional and national level. Trained personnel will be provided at each location to monitor and audit the commercial contracting. A full audit trail will be provided for activity for which payment by contractors is claimed. This will also implement the National Audit Office's recommendation 8 that, in an emergency, key financial controls must remain in place to ensure that monies are properly accounted for, that the risk of fraud and abuse are minimised and that value for money is secured as well as there being a clear audit trail with sufficient supporting documentation at all key stages.
LL R26 We recommend that the processes for procuring and delivering the necessary goods and services from external sources during a crisis be reviewed. Systems should be tested to ensure they can cope with unexpected increased demands. (p74)	<u>Accept.</u> Advice and guidance on procurement procedures, processes and practices and the availability of standard forms and contracts online will contribute to ensuring that the best commercial contracting practice can be developed and implemented immediately. Work on developing easily accessible best practice for commercial contracting and contract management in an emergency is well advanced. This will implement that part of the National Audit Office recommendation 3 for contingency plans to include the emergency purchasing of supplies and services as well as their recommendation 7 for clear procedures to be established for the procurement of supplies or services that are needed at very short notice.
LL R27 We recommend that priority be given to recruiting accounting and procurement professionals to operate in emergency control centres during a crisis. (p74)	<u>Accept.</u> Links have been established with other Government Departments, Local/Unitary Authorities, professional services companies, and specialist agencies to supply procurement professionals; quantity surveyors, contract managers, and accounting staff in an emergency. There will be close co-operation and links with the Scottish Executive and the Welsh Assembly Government.

RECOMMENDATION	RESPONSE
LL R28 We recommend that Defra revise its guidance and instructions for slaughter. (p78)	<u>Accept.</u> Defra has received comments from a number of field-based staff about slaughter instructions which will help it to identify the strengths and weaknesses of the current approach. Defra is currently reviewing the guidance on slaughter both for its own staff and for the slaughtermen they supervise.
LL R29 We recommend that as part of the mechanisms to trigger the wider Government response, the military be consulted at the earliest appropriate opportunity to provide advice and consider the nature of possible support. (p82)	<u>Accept.</u> The Contingency Plan requires that the Armed Forces will be alerted immediately a case of foot and mouth disease is confirmed. The main aim will be to ensure that the Armed Forces are fully informed and so are able to offer the most appropriate advice on their possible role.
LL R30 We recommend that as part of its contingency planning, Defra, the Scottish Executive and the National Assembly for Wales, working with the Civil Contingencies Secretariat, examine the practicality of establishing a national volunteer reserve trained and informed to respond immediately to an outbreak of Infectious animal disease. (p82)	<u>Accept.</u> The Cabinet Office is developing a protocol for managing the release by all Departments of staff for any Department dealing with a major incident or civil contingency. This is being developed as a Memorandum of Understanding. The Civil Contingencies Secretariat will also develop managers with skills suitable for managing emergencies, drawn from across Whitehall, who will be able to provide support either for their own Department or for others. These measures are designed to provide a flexible response to a range of possible challenges, rather than specifically an outbreak of animal disease. They will complement and support the contingency plans developed by each Department and Agency for those areas of public service for which they are responsible. Defra is seeking to identify people within Government Service who have the necessary skills and who would be willing to fill key posts in an animal disease emergency and those who would be available for wider administrative tasks. This will implement that part of the National Audit Office recommendation 3, which calls for contingency plans to include the deployment of staff. The Welsh Contingency Plan already identifies key individuals who would step into the breach in any future crisis.

RECOMMENDATION	RESPONSE
LL R31 We recommend that the National Assembly for Wales and Defra develop a comprehensive agreement for co-ordinating the management of outbreaks of infectious animal disease in Wales. This should cover all aspects of a disease outbreak, delegating responsibility locally, where appropriate, and providing clear lines of communication and accountability. (p84)	Accept. Defra and the Welsh Assembly Government will work to ensure effective communication and clear structures as part of their contingency plans. In so doing, regard will be had to the National Audit Office recommendation 2 for clear definitions of responsibility, reporting lines and accountability.

The Government is in discussion with the Welsh Assembly Government on the case for devolving further powers to it to deal with all future outbreaks of animal disease in Wales. |
| **LL R32** We recommend that, where the control of exotic animal diseases has wider economic or other implications, the Government ensure that those consequences for the country as a whole are fully considered. (p86) | Accept. The creation of Defra means that the interests of all sectors of the rural community can be brought together and considered in a joined-up way by a single Department. The Contingency Plan and the disease control strategies within it will have regard to the economic, financial and environmental impact of different methods of disease control, as recommended by the National Audit Office in their recommendation 2. |
| **LL R33** We recommend that contingency plans provide for early appointment of Regional Operations Directors or their equivalent to take on operational management of a crisis. There should be a cadre of senior managers - not all of whom need to come from central government - who can fulfil the role of the Regional Operations Director in an emergency and who should be trained in advance. (p87) | Accept. The Contingency Plan provides for the appointment of Regional Operations Directors (RODs) from the first day on which disease is confirmed. These posts and posts as managers of the administrative teams in Disease Control Centres, to be held on a contingency basis, are now being advertised in all government departments. A team of individuals have been identified to serve as RODs in the event of an immediate emergency.

Those selected will be required to familiarise themselves with their region and to take part in training exercises. |
| **LL R34** We recommend that Defra's Chief Scientist maintain a properly constituted standing committee ready to advise in an emergency on scientific aspects of disease control. The role of this group should include advising on horizon scanning and emerging risks. Particular attention should be given to the recommendations on the use of scientific advisory committees in the BSE inquiry report of 2000. (p91) | Accept. The Government agrees with this and Ministers have confirmed their wish to set up a new Science Advisory Council (SAC), as an advisory Non-Departmental Public Body, to provide advice to Defra's Chief Scientific Adviser on the scope, balance and direction of the Defra science spend. The SAC will be made up of senior and external scientists and, when it starts its work next year, it is expected to take a keen interest in the science programmes addressing livestock diseases. |

RECOMMENDATION	RESPONSE
	Defra has a horizon scanning research programme and a number of individual research programmes look at risk and emerging threats. Defra believes that its new Science Advisory Council should keep risk issues under close review when advising the Defra Chief Scientific Adviser on research programmes. They will also be tasked with setting up rapid and robust arrangements for advice in emergency circumstances. An interim Group has been established to provide advice until the full SAC is in place.
LL R35 We recommend that, from day one of an outbreak, provision be made to keep a record of all decisions made and any action to be taken. (p93)	Accept. Records of major decisions should be maintained and staff are aware of the importance of such action. This will be re-emphasised in the Contingency Plan.
LL R36 We recommend that the State Veterinary Service be routinely equipped with the most up-to-date diagnostic tools for use in clinical practice, to contribute to speed and certainty of action at critical times. (p95)	Accept. When validated diagnostic tests for field use become available Defra will ensure that the State Veterinary Service has access to them.
LL R37 We recommend that in order to build support steps always be taken to explain the rationale of policies on the ground, particularly where implementation is likely to be controversial. Wherever possible, local circumstances should be taken into account without undermining the overall strategy. (p98)	Accept. The Government has published a disease control (slaughter) protocol which indicates the circumstances in which particular policies would be applied and the reasons for them, so far as this is possible without knowing the precise circumstances of an individual outbreak. This is being discussed with stakeholders prior to its finalisation. The Government agrees that local circumstances must be taken into account, but believes that many aspects of policy have to be centrally defined, after the fullest possible consultation.
LL R38 We recommend that provision be made for the possible application of pre-emptive culling policies, if justified by well-informed veterinary scientific advice, and judged to be appropriate to the circumstances. (p99)	Accept. The Government welcomes endorsement of pre-emptive action as one option within a disease control strategy and believes that passage of the current Animal Health Bill would help to meet this recommendation.
LL R39 We recommend that a mechanism be put in place at the centre of government to assess potential domestic civil threats and emergencies and provide advice to the Prime Minister on when to trigger the wider response of Government. (p102)	Accept. A horizon scanning team has been established within the Civil Contingencies Secretariat to perform this function, closely linked to existing horizon scanning activity in Departments. The team has reported to No 10, Ministers and Departments through a senior level review committee since May 2002.

RECOMMENDATION	RESPONSE
LL R40 We recommend that, in future, a representative of the wider rural economy be invited to participate in the Joint Co-ordination Centre. (p106)	Accept. Defra is consulting the Countryside Agency on contingency planning and in particular to identify an appropriate representative from the wider rural community who would be invited to have a role within a future National Disease Control Centre. Representatives of Government Departments with an interest and other partners, including, where appropriate, stakeholders, will also be invited to have a presence.
LL R41 We recommend that the concept of a 'senatorial group' be developed to provide independent advice to the Prime Minister and Cabinet during national crises. (p107)	Accept in principle. The Government is considering possible methods of providing the Prime Minister and senior Ministers with support and strategic advice during crises. This would not replace the normal well-rehearsed crisis management machinery but would run alongside it, considering the strategy being followed and assisting in the elaboration of options for Ministers. It has yet to decide the best way of providing this support.
LL R42 We recommend that burning animals on mass pyres is not used again as a strategy for disposal. (p108)	Accept in principle. The Contingency Plan makes it clear that the disposal hierarchy expected to be used in any future crisis is: incineration; rendering; and licensed landfill. The level and availability of disposal capacity using these routes will be a factor in considering the optimum disease control strategy.
LL R43 We recommend that training for those with responsibility for managing disease control include the relevant legal frameworks and the structure and responsibilities of local government. (p112)	Accept. The Government agrees that State Veterinary Service staff must have an understanding of the structure and responsibilities of local government, and Defra is expanding on this in its training programme. All veterinary and technical staff should have received training on the work of local government within 12 months of appointment. This training will involve presentations from local government staff if possible, and subsequent feedback.
LL R44 We recommend that all agencies with responsibility for public health be actively involved in designing disease control strategies and in contingency planning and communications. (p122)	Accept. The Environment Agency, the Department of Health and the Food Standards Agency all have a major role in disease control strategies and their involvement in developing plans on a wide variety of issues including vaccination, communication and ground water authorisations is imperative. In addition, the UK

RECOMMENDATION	RESPONSE
	Zoonoses Group (UKZG) and the Surveillance Group on Diseases and Infections of Animals bring together the Government agencies involved in disease control. The UKZG will provide the new Health Protection Agency, the centrepiece of the Chief Medical Officer's infectious disease strategy, with advice and information on zoonoses.
LL R45 We recommend that local communities be consulted on mass disposal sites according to best practice guidelines, and that the question of compensation for communities accommodating emergency disposal sites be researched. We recognise that this is a complex legal area nationally and at EU level. (p114)	Further consideration. Defra will review the way any future disposal activities are likely to impact on local communities in the development of its contingency planning and local contingency plans will be drawn up in consultation with local stakeholders and community interests. The Contingency Plan makes it clear that the disposal hierarchy expected to be used in any future crisis is: incineration; rendering; and licensed landfill. Under these circumstances the Government does not consider compensation would be payable.
LL R46 We recommend that the Government consider the welfare implications of disease control policies, as part of contingency planning for FMD and other diseases, and seek to identify strategies that minimise the need for slaughter and disposal on welfare grounds. (p119)	Accept. The Government fully recognises that animal diseases, and the control measures which are adopted to tackle them, raise important animal welfare issues. It will not be possible to completely avoid collateral problems arising from, for example, movement freezes, and the Government agrees the need to plan against them so far as possible.
LL R47 We recommend that the Government establish a consensus on vaccination options for disease control in advance of an outbreak. (p129)	Accept. Defra will engage with stakeholders to try to establish as much common ground as possible prior to an outbreak on disease control strategies including vaccination.
LL R48 We recommend that the Government ensure the option of vaccination forms part of any future strategy for the control of FMD. (p129)	Accept. The Government agrees that the option of emergency vaccination should now be considered as part of the control strategy from the start of any outbreak of FMD.
LL R49 We recommend that the State Veterinary Service maintain the capability to vaccinate in the event of a future epidemic, if the conditions are right. (p129)	Accept. Defra is currently working to maintain and develop this vaccination capability.

RECOMMENDATION	RESPONSE
LL R50 We recommend that government make explicit the extent to which the wider effects of disease control strategies have been identified, measured and taken into account in policy decisions. (p137)	<u>Accept.</u> The Government will ensure that the wider effects of disease control policies are included in the risk assessments and cost benefit analyses of those policies and are reflected in the strategy for dealing with outbreaks.
LL R51 We recommend that the interests of all the sectors likely to bear the brunt of any costs be properly represented and taken into account when designing policy options to control animal disease outbreaks. (p139)	<u>Accept.</u> See Lessons Learned recommendation 32.
LL R52 We recommend that cost-benefit analyses on FMD control strategies should be updated and maintained. These should be undertaken at both the UK and EU level. (p139)	<u>Accept.</u> The Government will undertake such an analysis for the UK and will discuss this and other aspects of the inquiry reports with the Commission, with a view to ensuring that their lessons are fully learned at EU level.
LL R53 We recommend that the government build into its contingency plans the capacity to scale up communications systems and resources rapidly at the onset of any future outbreak if animal disease	<u>Accept.</u> Defra has worked with the Government Information and Communications Service (GICS) to ensure that the Department is better equipped to scale up its specialist communications staff resources. Additionally Defra maintains a list of freelance contacts and is drawing up a list of non press office staff within the Department who have useful communications skills and could be called on in a crisis. It is confident that in any future crisis, numbers could be rapidly escalated. The GICS News Co-ordination Centre is now well established and has protocols on increasing staff. These improvements deliver the National Audit Office recommendation 6 for communications and information systems to be reviewed by Defra to ensure that they would be able to cope in an emergency. The response to Lessons Learned recommendation 54 describes the position for Government as a whole.
LL R54 We recommend that a government-wide crisis communication strategy be developed by the Civil Contingencies Secretariat with specific plans being prepared at departmental level; for example by Defra and the devolved administrations in Scotland and Wales in the context of animal disease control. (p142)	<u>Accept.</u> The Civil Contingencies Secretariat (CCS) is working with Departments in a number of specific areas to enhance media and public communications strategies using a wide range of communication techniques including the Internet and the full resources of the Government Network in the regions. The CCS have tasked the Government News Network with developing networks of communication staff and emergency planners in a wide range of organisations throughout the country.

RECOMMENDATION	RESPONSE
	By their very nature strategies being developed now have to be relatively generic, but once an issue is raised, developing a specific communication strategy for it becomes a priority. In particular, the work being developed by the London Resilience Forum on media communications strategies in a major crisis will be used as a model for further work.
LL R55 We recommend that Defra develop its regional communication strategy and ensure that it has effective systems for disseminating clear and concise information quickly to all regional offices. This should be developed in the context of cross government crisis management planning, in consultation with the Regional Co-ordination Unit and Government Offices. (p143)	Accept. The Government accepts that this is an area where significantly more work is required. Defra has (compared with MAFF or DETR) many more agencies and non-departmental public bodies working at local level and a much wider rural proofing brief which requires a cross departmental communication of information. Defra has already enhanced its communications channels with regional operations, with greater co-ordination between the centre and Government Offices and Government News Network. Defra now has a dedicated team within its Press Office with sole responsibility for co-ordinating with Government News Network counterparts. A 'hub and spoke' system of information exchange with a central hub at HQ and communications "cells" in the regions is also planned.
	Communications in Wales will be the responsibility of the Welsh Assembly Government and in the development of contingency plans, Defra and the Assembly will ensure consistency of approach.
LL R56 We recommend that Defra resource its website to ensure that it is a state of the art operation. In any future outbreak, the website should be used extensively, and a central priority should be to ensure that it contains timely and up to date information at a national and local level. (p144)	Accept. Defra is reviewing its website under a wider communications strategy. The Department recognises the need for a resource which helps to transform the relationship and contact with customers and stakeholders and better integration between national and regional centres. An e-Communications Programme (e-CP) is in place to provide improved communications between Defra and its stakeholders, customers and the public and to provide a strategic approach to e-business which will allow this improvement in communications to continue through the longer term. A "New Media" team has been set up to bring a more cohesive approach to Defra's web presence. The aim is to increase electronic means of sharing more complete, accurate, and consistent information, with improved processes which are more effective and efficient.

Defra is aware that many farmers do not have direct access to the internet, and therefore does not intend to focus exclusively on the internet as a means of communications. Other older technologies will remain essential for the foreseeable future. One possibility which will be explored, is whether in a crisis, we could put out essential information on a set of teletext pages - to which many more farmers would have access.

The Welsh Assembly Government has created a new team to develop its website, drawing on experiences from last year's crisis.

LL R57 We recommend that Defra commission research into the effectiveness of its direct communications during the FMD outbreak of 2001 so that all the lessons may be learned, acted upon and the results published. (p144)

Accept. The Government agrees that finding out what people need to know is an essential part of the communications process. Defra undertook a research exercise in September 2001 asking farmers and the public what their main sources of information on FMD were, and seeking their views on what information they would want in the future. Further research was carried out in January 2002 into how Defra communicates with farmers more generally, what they want from Defra, and how Defra can meet that need. The results have been used in formulating the overall Communications Strategy, which will be published shortly.

LL R58 We recommend that the State Veterinary Service revise all its disease control forms A-E and information about exotic diseases in liaison with the Plain English Campaign.

Accept. These forms will be revised when the Foot and Mouth Order 1983 is consolidated and updated. The need for plain English will be taken fully into account. The State Veterinary service will, in addition, be reviewing its internal and external communications.

LL R59 We recommend that communications strategies during a crisis take special account of the needs of the International media. (p147)

Accept. Defra is making efforts to keep its overseas Environment and Agriculture attaches better informed. In addition, Defra has discussed with the Foreign Press Association and the London correspondents section of the Foreign and Commonwealth Office ways to establish closer links with international media to improve responses to foreign media issues. London based correspondents for foreign media are included in circulation and contact lists and invited to take part in Defra lobby briefings.

RECOMMENDATION	RESPONSE

LL R60 We recommend that farmers, vets and others involved in the livestock industry have access to training in biosecurity measures. Such training should form an integral part of courses at agricultural colleges. (p148)

Accept in principle. Defra and the National Assembly for Wales Agriculture Department (NAWAD) have written to the agricultural colleges to draw their attention to recommendation 60 and 72 so they can reflect on the specific biosecurity needs in their syllabuses.

The Government will ensure that the need for biosecurity training is addressed in the programme which takes forward the commitment, announced on 26 March 2002, to review the effectiveness of training and education for farmers and other land managers. The review will include skills issues within a broader customer-focussed programme of work, looking at advice and information services as well as access to learning provision for land managers and other occupational groups in rural areas. (See also Lessons Learned recommendation 61)

For vets Defra is developing a biosecurity training module with the aim that:

- All State Veterinary Service (SVS) field staff are competent to a specified level in biosecurity measures

- Field staff new to the SVS to have initial training in biosecurity measures within 1 month of joining.

- The training module in biosecurity measures is readily available for use for all staff drafted in to assist with emergency disease situations.

Once the module is developed, it could be assessed for suitability and possible adaptation for Veterinary Colleges to use if they wished.

LL R61 We recommend that the livestock industry and government jointly develop codes of practice on biosecurity. They should explore ways to communicate effectively with all practitioners and how incentives might be used to raise standards. (p150)

Accept. The Government issued a one-page summary code on biosecurity against FMD to all livestock farmers in August 2002 which had the endorsement of parties including livestock organisations.

Work on biosecurity codes relating to the possible incursion of exotic disease for farmers and others associated with the livestock industry need to be integrated into a wider framework of biosecurity measures, as the Government is keen to find new ways of improving biosecurity, and will investigate alternative approaches which might be employed to raise awareness. This will include investigation of what incentives might be employed to raise standards.

In Wales, ministers have produced 10 biosecurity commandments which have been sent to all livestock farmers in Wales.

LL R62 We recommend that the use of Restricted Infected Area ('Blue Box' biosecurity arrangements) procedures be built into contingency plans. (p160)

Accept. Provision for Restricted Infected Areas is in the Contingency Plan. The Government fully accepts the importance of rigorous enforcement of biosecurity controls from the earliest stages of an epidemic. However, the detailed application of Infected Area controls has to be reviewed in the light of resource and personnel constraints in all the public bodies involved.

This focus on biosecurity measures will ensure that any necessary action is taken under the National Audit Office recommendation 10.2 that research should be undertaken into the efficiency of biosecurity measures.

LL R63 We recommend that disease control policies be developed in consultation with those local authorities responsible for implementing them.(p153)

Accept. The Department strengthened its relations with the local authority community throughout FMD and its aftermath and this will be maintained. The status of local authorities as key partners in the animal health sphere will be reflected in closer consultation over policies.

LL R64 We recommend that the UK urge the OIE to consider the implications, for the detection and control of FMD, of the removal of swine vesicular disease from the List A of Notifiable diseases. (p156)

Accept. Swine Vesicular Disease (SVD) in its clinical form is difficult to distinguish from FMD. Removal of SVD from the OIE List A would have national and international consequences for the control of these vesicular diseases.

LL R65 We recommend that the Pirbright Laboratory resources, and research programmes, be integrated into the national strategy for animal disease control, and budget provisions be made accordingly. (p159)

Accept. The Government will consider how best to use the available facilities for surveillance and research into animal diseases in developing the Animal Health and Welfare Strategy and the Veterinary Surveillance Strategy. Clearly, any such strategic approach to laboratories will need to take due account of the facilities at Pirbright.

LL R66 The State Veterinary Service, together with the Pirbright Laboratory, should increase their horizon scanning and threat assessment capabilities for major infectious animal diseases. (p160)

Accept. The Government will take this forward through its Veterinary Surveillance Strategy. This will address the enhancement and prioritisation of 'horizon scanning' for new or changing disease threats. This will include working in partnership with the relevant national Reference Laboratories which in the case of FMD, is the Pirbright Laboratory.

RECOMMENDATION	RESPONSE
LL R67 We recommend that in developing the surveillance strategy, there be the widest possible involvement of those with a role to play in surveillance. (p160)	Accept. In his foreword to the report on veterinary surveillance by Meah & Lewis (2000) the Minister for Agriculture, the Rt. Hon Nick Brown MP, said that he wanted to see a realistic strategy for veterinary surveillance which meets the needs of Government, the general public, industry and health and veterinary professionals. He also emphasised that the strategy development process should be as open and inclusive as possible. During development of the Veterinary Surveillance Strategy, a wide range of stakeholders will be consulted, including those who have a role to play.
LL R68 We recommend that Defra and the Department for Education and Skills jointly explore with the veterinary professional bodies and higher education institutions the scope for increasing the capacity of undergraduate and postgraduate veterinary provision. Equivalent work should be done in Scotland and Wales. (p160)	Further consideration. Discussions took place in 1999 between MAFF and the Department for Education and Skills on the number of veterinary surgeon graduates leaving UK veterinary schools. The numbers are continuing to increase and it is questionable whether there is a shortage of vets available for work in the UK. Defra is opening further discussions with DfES and other professional bodies and will explore veterinary training issues. The Government accepts that it is essential that vets are encouraged to join the State Veterinary Service (SVS) by providing a good career structure including a comprehensive Continual Professional Development framework of post-graduate and other training and development. Defra is working with veterinary colleges to promote the work of the SVS and to increase a practitioner's knowledge of state veterinary medicine. In particular it is setting up pilot programmes and training days. Defra is also liaising with the colleges as part of its review of the relationship between the SVS and private vets.
LL R69 We recommend that Government develop opportunities for increased use of veterinary 'paramedics'. (p160)	Accept. The Government accepts that it should look at ways of further developing opportunities for the increased use of veterinary para-professionals. Part of the Government's Action Plan for farming made a commitment to review the scope for properly trained and regulated para-professionals to undertake certain activities that the Veterinary Surgeons' Act currently restricts to vets.

RECOMMENDATION	RESPONSE
	Defra has asked the Royal College of Veterinary Surgeons, for its views on the use of para-professionals.
	Defra needs to assess both current and future needs and evaluate the role that para-professionals may be able to play within those needs before any conclusions can be reached.
LL R70 We recommend as many functions of the State Veterinary Service as possible be relocated from London, to regional centres, particularly to Scotland and Wales. (p161)	Further consideration. Within England Defra recognises that there are difficulties in attracting staff to posts in the South East, particularly in the London headquarters. State Veterinary Service operational work has to be carried out locally and cannot be transferred to other parts of the country. However, a new approach of partnership working between policy teams and operational staff will increase the contribution of field based staff to policy formulation. This may help to alleviate some of the pressures in HQ. The links between the SVS and the Devolved Administrations in Scotland and Wales have also been strengthened.
LL R71 We recommend that Government support a national action group charged with the responsibility of producing a plan to tackle the gaps in practitioners' knowledge of preventing and managing infectious diseases of livestock. To be effective this will need a timetable, milestones for achievement and incentives. (p161)	Not accepted in this form. Defra will be involving stakeholders in the course of its consideration of the Animal Health and Welfare Strategy, which will need to address failure to prevent and manage diseases of farmed livestock. The recommendations of the Lessons Learned Inquiry will be borne in mind, but the Animal Health and Welfare Strategy will not necessarily recommend a national action group.
LL R72 We recommend that colleges, universities and training organisations provide courses to equip those working in the food and livestock Industries, and those owning susceptible animals, with the skills and knowledge to enable them to recognise the signs of animal disease early and take appropriate action to prevent its spread. (p161)	Accept in principle. See response to Lessons Learned recommendation 60.
LL R73 We recommend that Defra commission a handbook for farmers on identifying and responding to animal disease, drawing on the experience of 2001. (p162)	Accept in principle. The Government will consider how to get the message across effectively to farmers on how to recognise and respond to the notifiable diseases in conjunction with the farming unions and other trade associations. This will include the use of the internet, e-learning and pamphlets.

RECOMMENDATION	RESPONSE
LL R74 We recommend that training for local Veterinary Inspectors in exotic diseases be intensified, and consolidated into ongoing training strategies. (p162)	Accept. See the response to Lessons Learned recommendation 3.
LL R75 We recommend that farm assurance schemes take account of animal health and welfare, biosecurity, food safety and environmental issues. (p162)	Further consideration. Defra, the Scottish Executive Environment and Rural Affairs Department and National Assembly for Wales Agriculture Department have written to the main assurance schemes operating in Great Britain to draw their attention to recommendation 75, and to seek information on the animal health and biosecurity standards that apply in their schemes and what plans they have for reviewing these in the light of the recommendation. This information will be considered in the context of the development of the Animal Health and Welfare Strategy and the development of other policies.
LL R76 We recommend that the livestock industry work with Government to undertake a thorough review of the assurance and licensing options to identify those arrangements most likely to reward good practice and take-up of training, and how such a new system might be implemented. (p162)	Further consideration. The Government is keen to work with industry in this area. Like the Policy Commission on the Future of Food and Farming, which favours a Whole Farm approach to regulation rather than licensing, at this stage the Government does not think that there is a need to license livestock farmers. (See also Lessons Learned recommendation 75)
LL R77 We recommend that the powers available in the Animal Health Act 1981 be re-examined, possibly in the context of a wider review of animal health legislation, to remove any ambiguity over the legal basis for future disease control strategies. (p163)	Accept. The Government does not consider the Animal Health Act powers to be "ambiguous". But it agrees that they could be strengthened in relation to some aspects of disease control - notably pre-emptive culling and powers of entry for emergency vaccination - which the inquiries firmly endorse. The Government believes that the passage of the current Animal Health Bill will help meet part of the Inquiry recommendation. The Government will address the scope and nature of future legislation next year following publication of the Animal Health and Welfare Strategy. This is likely to involve rationalisation of existing regulation, covering such issues as encouraging better biosecurity, harmonising systems of compensation and risk sharing as between industry and taxpayer. This takes forward the National Audit Office recommendation 11 for the review of current animal health legislation to ensure that it meets current and likely requirements for dealing with an outbreak of FMD.

RECOMMENDATION	RESPONSE
LL R78 We recommend that the Government retain the 20 day movement restrictions pending a detailed risk assessment and wide ranging cost-benefit analysis. (p164)	Accept. The Government has commissioned comprehensive risk assessments and cost benefit analyses, as recommended by the inquiry reports, to inform decisions as to the controls to be applied to animal movements in the absence of an FMD outbreak.
LL R79 We recommend that Government develop a comprehensive livestock tracing system using electronic tags to cover cattle, sheep and pigs taking account of developments at EU level. The Government should seek to lead the debate in Europe on this issue. (p164)	Accept in principle. The Government agrees that the FMD crisis underlined the importance of having effective systems of livestock identification and tracing in place. Electronic identification of each animal together with electronic data transfer of the information captured on farm to a central database is likely to be the way ahead. However, technological advances are needed before industry-wide implementation is possible. The views of the European Commission are also needed, as it is important that any new systems are developed on an EU-wide harmonised basis to encourage international trade. An industry/Defra steering group has been set up together with the Livestock Identification and Tracing Programme to resolve implementation issues and to take the work forward. Meanwhile, interim measures are being put in place to improve tracing of sheep, pigs and goats, through licensing and recording of batch movements.
LL R80 We recommend that the joint Defra Industry Working Group for Animal Disease Insurance ensure that its scope and membership is set widely enough to address valuation and compensation issues highlighted by the 2001 outbreak. Clear deadlines should be set for reporting progress. (p165)	Accept. Defra accepts that these two topics are closely inter-related and thus the approach to new policy initiatives for both has been integrated.
	The linkage between work on an animal disease levy/insurance scheme with an on-going review of compensation arrangements is already well established. There is a clear need to rationalise the current fragmented approach to compensation for animal diseases as a whole, not only to simplify the mechanism, but also to speed up and introduce predictability in the process of valuation, in the event of disease outbreaks.
	One of the options being considered, for an animal disease levy, would raise funds from industry, in advance, to cover about half of the anticipated costs of outbreaks of certain exotic diseases, including compensation. The cost of compensation will clearly influence estimates of the funds to be raised. In order to calculate levy rates in a way that ensures fairness and equity, it is necessary to have a clear policy on valuation and compensation.

RECOMMENDATION	RESPONSE
	Proposals for a fundamental overhaul of animal disease compensation arrangements and for an animal disease levy/insurance scheme are being developed simultaneously. Defra will consult widely before implementing any proposals. The results of these consultations will be reported to the joint Defra Industry Working Group on Animal Disease Insurance. The review of compensation payments is also recommended by the National Audit Office (their recommendation 9).
LL R81 We recommend that Defra develop further its interim plan, published in March 2002, in full consultation with all interested parties. Its relevance should be maintained through agreed programmes of rehearsal, practice, review and reporting. This work should be given priority for funding. (p165)	Accept. Progress has already been made on developing the FMD Contingency Plan which will be placed on the Defra website on the day this response is published. The Plan now takes account of the inquiries' recommendations and will be reviewed and updated with input from interested parties and following training exercises and testing. It will remain as a "living document" and be updated as necessary. Provision has been made in the 2002 Spending Review for contingency planning to be taken forward. In so doing, regard will be had to the National Audit Office recommendation 2 for clear definitions of responsibility, reporting lines and accountability. In drawing up the Plan, Defra will, in line with National Audit Office recommendation 4, consult central and local government, farmers and other stakeholders. The process of regular testing and review of the Plan is also recommended by the NAO (their recommendation 5). Similar steps are being taken by the Welsh Assembly Government.

Royal Society Key Findings

KEY FINDING	RESPONSE
Key Finding 1 The overall objective of policy must be to minimise the risk of a disease entering the country and, if it does enter, to ensure the outbreak is localised and does not develop into an epidemic. (vii)	Accept. The Government's Action Plan on imports is intended to address this issue and improved veterinary surveillance will also assist the early detection and eradication of outbreaks of disease. In addition, the Government intends to put in place proportionate controls over animal movements in "peacetime" and to encourage farmers to raise standards of biosecurity.
Key Finding 2 The UK, and the EU, should seek to retain *"disease free"* status with respect to FMD and the other most serious infectious diseases. Under present circumstances, this status should be "disease-free without (routine) vaccination". But this proviso could change if, for example, the risk of an outbreak occurring increased sharply, better vaccines became available or the trading regulations associated with disease-free status were further changed, so it must be kept under active review. (vii)	Accept. The Government agrees that the UK should aim to keep its disease-free without routine vaccination trade status.
Key Finding 3 Better contingency planning is vital. The Government must be empowered to act decisively during an outbreak. This requires prior debate about the control measures to be adopted. The Government's Contingency Plans should therefore be brought before Parliament for debate and approval. The Plans should be subject to a practical rehearsal each year and should be formally reviewed triennially to ensure that they take account of: the latest information about the scale of international disease threat; changes in farming practice; scientific and technological developments; regulatory developments at national, EU and global level; and the country's state of preparedness. (vii)	Accept in part. Detailed contingency planning for both the national and local response to an outbreak is now taking place. The plans will be "living" documents and will be kept up to date through regular rehearsals and reviews covering different scenarios and areas. They will be formally reviewed at least triennially.

The Government will provide the Contingency Plans to the Select Committee for Environment Food and Rural Affairs and will lay them before Parliament once further work and testing has taken place. The need for a debate in Parliament will be kept under review.

The Welsh Assembly Government are developing their own contingency plans. |

KEY FINDING	RESPONSE
Key Finding 4 As a result of globalisation, the risk of invasion by exotic (i.e. non-endemic) animal diseases has increased. It is essential that the UK, and the EU, strengthen their *early warning systems* and ensure that warnings are acted upon. This requires an EU risk and surveillance unit; better funding for the OIE reference laboratories to track disease spread and type the strains; heightened animal disease surveillance on farms; and greater interaction between farmers and veterinarians to improve the effectiveness of national surveillance. Import controls over meat products require tightening. (vii)	Accept in part. The global situation with regard to the occurrence of FMD and other diseases, particularly with regard to its third country trading partners, is monitored closely by both the EU Commission and the UK either through direct contacts with third countries, via the Office International des Epizooties (OIE) or through the Food and Agriculture Organisation EU Commission on FMD.

The Government accepts the need to support OIE reference laboratories but the mandate given to these laboratories reflects their international not national obligations. Furthermore, controls for exotic diseases are harmonised across the Community and specifically require that Member States designate and support national reference laboratories. The Government accepts the need to support national reference laboratories so they can fully meet all their obligations, including where this is necessary, their OIE reference laboratory functions.

The Government agrees on the need to review its surveillance activities and is doing so through its development of a national Veterinary Surveillance Strategy that will encompass farmers, vets and all those involved in this area. To date five strategic goals have been identified. The first of these is to strengthen collaborations between the providers, users and beneficiaries of veterinary surveillance. The importance of the interaction between farmers and vets has been recognised and a pilot study is planned to identify the best use of practising veterinary surgeons in surveillance activities. The training of Local Veterinary Inspectors, and their potential contribution to surveillance is also under review. Good progress is being made on a considerable programme of action on illegal imports.

KEY FINDING	RESPONSE
Key Finding 5 Routine vaccination against some of the OIE List A diseases is possible. While there are no overwhelming scientific or economic reasons against this approach being adopted we believe that, at present, the considerable technical problems and the trade implications argue against changing the current arrangements. Nevertheless it is clear that the long-term solution is to develop a vaccine against FMD (and other diseases such as classical swine fever) that confers lifelong sterile immunity against all strains of the virus. An international research effort is required to develop such a vaccine. (vii)	<u>Accept in principle.</u> The Government agrees that an improved vaccine that would permit routine and global vaccination of livestock against all strains of FMD is a desirable long-term goal. This is an issue of international rather than national scope and would be most effectively led by an international organisation such as the Food and Agriculture Organisation or possibly as an EU initiative. This issue will be raised in discussions on future research with our EU partners.
Key Finding 6 The precautionary principle should be adopted more widely to ensure that any disease outbreak cannot develop into an epidemic. One of the most effective ways of achieving this is to minimise animal movements at all times. The Government should consider a system whereby early warning infection triggers significantly enhanced precautionary measures. (vii)	<u>Accept.</u> Proportionate controls over animal movements will apply in the absence of an outbreak and once a case is confirmed the Contingency Plan allows for a national movement ban to be imposed while the extent of the outbreak is ascertained. Restricted Infected Area Controls would be imposed around the Infected Premises.
Key Finding 7 Rapid culling of infected premises and known dangerous contacts, combined with movement control and rapid diagnosis, will remain essential to controlling FMD and most other highly infectious diseases. In many cases this will not be sufficient guarantee that the outbreak does not develop into an epidemic. Given recent advances in vaccine science and improved trading regulations, *emergency vaccination* should now be considered as part of the control strategy from the start of any outbreak of FMD. By this we mean vaccination-to-live, under which meat and meat products from animals vaccinated and subsequently found to be uninfected may enter the normal human food chain. The Government should prepare the regulatory framework and practical arrangements (e.g. validation of tests, and the supply of vaccines) that would allow this. There must at the outset be an exit strategy agreed among the main stakeholders to allow the country to return to the preferred "disease-free without vaccination" status. (viii)	<u>Accept.</u> Emergency vaccination should now be considered as part of the control strategy from the start of any outbreak of FMD where measures additional to culling of infected animals and dangerous contacts are needed. The Government also agrees that where emergency vaccination is used this should be to live wherever possible, and is committed to tackling the issues identified by the Royal Society which need to be resolved to make this a fully viable disease control strategy.

KEY FINDING	RESPONSE

Key Finding 8 The first suspected case in an outbreak must be diagnosed in an approved OIE reference laboratory. Thereafter, *modern diagnostic methods* – including pen-side tests – need to be developed that can shift the burden of diagnosis to veterinarians on the farm. Rapid diagnosis, particularly before clinical signs appear, would limit the size of any epidemic and improve strategic deployment of resources. Such diagnostic methods must be linked by modern telecommunications to central headquarters. (viii)

Accept in part. Directive 85/511/EEC as amended requires that the first suspected case of FMD is diagnosed in an approved national laboratory. In the case of the UK, this is the Institute for Animal Health at Pirbright, which is also an OIE-approved laboratory and the Food and Agriculture Organisation world reference laboratory. Thereafter the confirmation of further cases is based on a combination of clinical findings and any known epidemiological link to other infected premises. Defra would not normally confirm disease on clinical grounds in a farm that is in a "clean county" and where there is no link to another infected premises. In such cases Defra would value and slaughter the "clinical cases" and submit samples to the laboratory before confirming disease if the samples are positive.

Hence the burden of diagnosis has always been, and should remain, predominantly with the field vet. It is agreed however that anything that speeds up the ability to obtain results of tests rapidly in cases of equivocal or non-apparent clinical signs is a substantial asset. The development and use of pen side tests would help providing that they are sensitive, specific and robust and able to detect the disease at all stages, dependable in the local environment and situation, and not require valuable resource to continually monitor the suspect animals. It would not remove the need for adequate biosecurity or restrictions, or sound clinical judgement on site. The government agrees that the notification of such results to the central headquarters must use the latest technology and this will be examined.

Key Finding 9   There is considerable benefit to be gained from understanding the quantitative aspects of infectious disease dynamics. *Quantitative modelling* is one of the essential tools both for developing strategies in preparation for an outbreak and for predicting and evaluating the effectiveness of control policies during an outbreak. A prerequisite is a central database incorporating improved data on farms, the location of animals, animal movements, and the characteristics of the diseases, together with arrangements to input disease control data in a timely and assured way during an outbreak. More work is required to refine the existing models and to strengthen their capacity to inform policy, which in turn requires full access by researchers to this database and to the data on previous outbreaks. (viii)

Accept. Modelling was used to good effect during the 2001 epidemic and has a vital role in the development of disease control strategy and during epidemics. On 23rd May 2002 Defra held a workshop with leading modellers and is actively considering future needs. (See Royal Society recommendations 3.2 and 6.1 for more detail).

Key Finding 10   A national strategy for animal disease research should be developed. The overall costs of animal diseases to the UK over the last fifteen years may well have exceeded £15 billion: research is the only rational means available of improving animal health and diminishing disease. The strategy should be delivered through a "virtual national centre for animal disease research and surveillance" involving the Institute for Animal Health, the Veterinary Laboratories Agency and research groups in universities. It should also involve private research institutes and publicly funded animal disease research being undertaken in Northern Ireland and Scotland. (viii)

Accept in part. The Government agrees that co-ordination of research could be strengthened further and is committed to preparing a national Animal Health and Welfare Strategy. During this process Defra will engage with the widest possible interests in its preparation including research institutes, agencies, academics, public and private funders and industry. A significant outcome will be the identification of research requirements for both surveillance and animal disease. Equally research findings will feed back into the Strategy.

An important element of the new Animal Health and Welfare Strategy is the development of a strategy for enhancing veterinary surveillance in the UK. One of the strategic goals so far identified in an early draft of the strategy is the development of a transparent and open process for prioritising surveillance activities. A key component of this is the collation of information relating to diseases or conditions for which surveillance is to be maintained into "profiles". Relevant information includes epidemiological information about the disease and the availability of suitable diagnostic tests. Collation of such information will facilitate the identification of important gaps in knowledge, and enable the research work needed to fill these gaps to be identified and prioritised. See reference to Royal Society recommendations 10.1, 10.2 and 10.3.

Royal Society Recommendations

RECOMMENDATION	RESPONSE
RS R1.1 The UK Government should bring before Parliament for debate a framework for the Contingency Plans covering the principles involved in handling outbreaks of infectious exotic diseases and the resources required for their implementation. (p1)	<u>Accept in part.</u> The Government will provide the Contingency Plans to the Select Committee for Environment Food & Rural Affairs and will lay them before Parliament once further work and testing has taken place. The need for a debate in Parliament will be kept under review.
RS R1.2 The Prime Minister should establish a formal procedure to review at three-yearly intervals: ● the level of threat from imported animal diseases of livestock ● changes in livestock farming practices that could affect vulnerability to disease ● scientific and therapeutic advances that could affect policy options ● the UK's and Europe's state of preparedness. (p1)	<u>Accept in principle.</u> The Government accepts the need for a regular review of the threat and the response capability - and (as the Lessons Learned report has proposed) a regular public report. Precise mechanism and ownership need to be considered further. The views of stakeholders will be taken during consultation on the Animal Health and Welfare Strategy.
RS R1.3 The UK should continue to strive for "disease-free" status against highly infectious diseases such as those listed in the OIE's List A. (p5)	<u>Accept.</u> The Government welcomes this recommendation. The Royal Society report demonstrates why disease-free status is important to the country.
RS R1.4 Providing the level of international threat does not increase; there are improved import controls; and there is a demonstrable improvement in the arrangements for handling disease outbreaks, the UK should not adopt a policy of routine vaccination, and should retain the internationally recognised status of "disease-free without vaccination". (p6)	<u>Accept.</u> The Government recognises the strength of the Royal Society's caveats on improved import controls and handling of disease outbreaks.
RS R3.1 Defra should undertake a systematic analysis of the information available on the relative threats to the UK from the range of diseases covered here (and other significant diseases such as TSEs and TB), taking account of the impact of globalisation and climate change, in order to set priorities for the national strategy for animal disease and surveillance. (p35)	<u>Accept.</u> Defra proposes that the Veterinary Surveillance Strategy should include the development of a transparent and open prioritisation system which will use information collected about the major diseases or conditions, including other factors which might affect the level of endemic disease or the likelihood of an exotic disease incursion. The Strategy will also consider what surveillance is necessary for factors which may change the risk of a disease occurring, such as changes in vector distribution, is necessary.

RECOMMENDATION	RESPONSE
RS R3.2 Defra should undertake a comprehensive review of the available information on FMD and develop a consistent and coherent database of the basic information that would be required during an outbreak. **(p35)**	Accept. Defra accepts the need to ensure information is available. Work continues on collecting and reviewing information on FMD from this outbreak and others around the world. (see Royal Society recommendation 6.1 for more detail) Work is also underway within Defra and the Welsh Assembly Government to develop a comprehensive family of associated databases which will link businesses to both land and animals. Disease control systems will draw from this core data.
RS R3.3 Defra should carry out urgent research into local transmission of FMD that will improve biosecurity in the field. **(p35)**	Accept. Local transmission of FMD virus during the 2001 UK outbreak was pronounced and the probable cause of the introduction of virus to 78% of premises that became infected. Extensive epidemiological data was collected in all areas and is suitable for further study into the mechanisms of disease transfer. This data already establishes that good biosecurity was of critical importance. It is well recognised that the enhanced biosecurity adopted in the Blue Boxes (Restricted Infected Areas) reduced the local spread of infection in those areas. There are currently studies underway concerning the methods of local spread, the susceptible stock involved, and the particular risk factors associated with dairy herds.

RECOMMENDATION	RESPONSE
RS R5.1 Defra should propose an EU-wide risk assessment unit and centralised database on surveillance and disease data, and a review of the bodies that provide early warning of animal disease threats. (p54)	<u>Accept in principle.</u> Defra is working closely with the European Commission to support initiatives to protect against further incursions of disease, such as the revised FMD Directive and new rules to control personal imports. Defra is committed to sharing with the Commission the outcome of the current Risk Assessment on the introduction of FMD in imports. The possibility of a central EU risk assessment unit should be considered in the light of our experience.
	In the UK Defra is developing an Information Management System to receive information reported to Defra on new disease outbreaks in livestock and poultry from around the world. It is being actively used to log documents, track diseases and proactively distribute information within Defra. It is linked to a Geographical Information System which provides mapping outputs used to inform risk assessments. In the future this capability will be extended to provide electronic, interactive maps for the whole of Defra.
RS R5.2 Defra should promote the speedy implementation of the Action Plan on illegal importing and of a much more co-ordinated approach at all levels by all bodies concerned with import control. (p54)	<u>Accept.</u> A considerable programme of action on imports is already underway, with Defra in the lead. Following a Cabinet Office study, all activity against smuggling of meat, animal products, fish and plant matter will be brought together in HM Customs & Excise and backed by a new dedicated target in Customs for service delivery in this area. There will be substantially improved co-ordination between the main control agencies, and between these agencies and Customs, under the oversight of a new ministerial group. The Government will also seek a step-change in the coordination and delivery of local authority inspection of imported foodstuffs and products of animal origin at ports within one year. Thereafter the Government will then look hard again at the case for bringing these functions from local authorities into a central agency, or delivering them from other routes.
	Defra will re-examine the Action Plan later this year.

RECOMMENDATION	RESPONSE
RS R5.3 Defra should investigate all the issues connected with reducing animal movements and come forward with practicable solutions that strike the right balance between the legitimate interests of livestock owners, market systems and long-term disease control. (p54)	<u>Accept.</u> The Government has commissioned comprehensive risk assessments and cost benefit analyses, as recommended by the inquiry reports, to inform decisions as to the controls to be applied to animal movements in the absence of an outbreak.
RS R5.4 Defra should ensure that all keepers of livestock (including that not kept for food production) are properly registered and submit to Defra each year the name of their nominated private veterinary surgeon and a health plan approved by the same veterinary surgeon. (P54)	<u>Further consideration.</u> The benefits of this proposal from the point of view of animal health and welfare will need to be weighed against the costs of the additional regulation. Defra will need to find the right way of ensuring that all those involved with livestock have a responsible approach to their care, have an understanding of the serious diseases to look out for, and make sensible use of professional veterinary services. A whole farm approach encouraging farmers to plan good animal health practice into their every day husbandry activities will help to achieve this.
RS R5.5 Defra should establish an Applied Research Unit on Livestock Management Practices that will undertake or commission research leading to (i) the design of effective biosecurity measures against infectious animal diseases, and (ii) the design of livestock management structures and practices that improve animal health in terms of infectious diseases. (p55)	<u>Accept in principle.</u> The Government recognises that more needs to be done to secure the health of UK livestock and actions are in hand. Resources are already in place to diagnose and respond to exotic microbial infections, such as FMD and rabies, and further research is supported at the Institute for Animal Health and Veterinary Laboratory Agency to improve diagnosis and prophylaxis. Defra uses the advice from this research base when designing effective biosecurity measures. Defra's Livestock Science Unit and the Scottish Executive Environment and Rural Affairs Department support research into livestock management practices that will improve the ability of animals to resist infectious disease challenge. Current research programmes valued at over £10.5 million are pursuing these objectives. Defra plans to have recommendations for improved management practice from 2005. Implementation of effective livestock management practice to reduce disease transmission will require the involvement and support of the UK livestock industry. A consultation is underway to seek stakeholder views on the establishment of a new research Priorities Board, recommended by the Policy

RECOMMENDATION	RESPONSE

Commission on the Future of Farming and Food. A Priorities Board would provide a forum for stakeholders across the livestock industry to consider options for improving management practice to reduce disease transmission. Defra will study the inquiry recommendations in detail to assess whether a more formal structure is required to progress research in this area.

RS R6.1 Defra should establish a review to determine the data required for informing policy both before and during epidemics of infectious diseases. This review should involve all those likely to be involved in disease control, including modelling teams, and cover:

- information to be collected on a routine basis, and how this can be kept up to date;

- information to be collected during an outbreak

- incorporation of the data into a central database

- use of modern techniques for real time data capture and verification. (p72)

Accept. Early on in his work Sir Brian Follett indicated to the Chief Veterinary Officer that a meeting of all those involved in modelling and disease control should be established. Defra held a meeting on 23rd May 2002 with such a group and discussed what information should be collected and what models were needed. The meeting report has been published on the Defra website: http://www.defra.gov.uk/research/Publications/default.htm. Defra is actively considering future needs.

The State Veterinary Service (SVS) is currently developing disease control systems to aid the management of both endemic diseases and outbreaks of exotic diseases. The scoping studies for these systems will address such issues by analysing the business and information requirements of such systems. Pilot studies and field trials to investigate the feasibility of providing SVS field staff with mobile IT facilities such as laptops and personal digital assistants to enhance the efficiency, quality and effectiveness of their day to day work and real-time data collection are also occurring.

In addition, Defra is currently developing a veterinary surveillance system which will bring together background information on livestock populations and their locations, overlaid with numerator data about incidents of diseases, infections, intoxications etc. The database will also include data and parameters taken from peer reviewed disease profiles. Analysis of this will provide a means of monitoring the effectiveness of existing control or preventative measures and can be invaluable in deciding the feasibility of attempting an eradication programme. Equally, surveillance of certain parameters can give an indirect means of monitoring significant issues that change the risk or likelihood of disease occurrence and will help to target surveillance at particular times or places.

RECOMMENDATION	RESPONSE
	The development of this system is occurring in collaboration with surveillance stakeholders and a programme of stakeholder workshops was held in October 2002.
RS R6.2 Defra should commission research to improve the methodology used to identify dangerous contacts. (p72)	<u>Further consideration.</u> Defra will study the Royal Society's recommendations in detail to assess, as part of its research strategy and the Animal Health and Welfare Strategy, what research work is required to address this recommendation.
RS R6.3 Defra should undertake a major research programme into the potential of mathematical modelling for understanding the quantitative aspects of animal disease. Mathematical models can be used both in preparing for outbreaks (including evaluating alternative strategies) and during the course of controlling an epidemic. (p72)	<u>Further consideration.</u> Early on in his work Sir Brian Follett indicated to the Chief Veterinary Officer that a meeting of all those involved in modelling and disease control should be established. See Royal Society recommendation 6.1. A range of models was identified. Defra will use the information that came from this meeting and study the Royal Society recommendations in detail to assess what research work is required to address them.
RS R6.4 Defra should ensure that the data from the 2001 epidemic are checked and then made widely available, while ensuring that any data protection issues are resolved. (p72)	<u>Accept.</u> Data from the 2001 epidemic is being cleansed; Defra envisages alerting the scientific community to the data that is available, and inviting concept notes. Data protection is an issue, but should be manageable.
RS R7.1 Defra should consult with other member states to ensure that the OIE is appropriately constituted to validate new diagnostic techniques and reagents as rapidly as possible; and that OIE reference laboratories are supported politically and financially so they can better undertake their national and international obligations, including the development of diagnostic tests. (p84)	<u>Accept.</u> The Office International des Epizooties (OIE), through its Standards Commission, sets down standards for tests used to underpin international trade and control disease. As such it already has a mechanism for evaluating diagnostic tests and reagents. New standards are ratified annually at the OIE General Session by all OIE member states. As OIE members, all EU Member States contribute to discussions on OIE standards and guidelines and the UK will consult with its EU partners about the validation process.
	OIE laboratories have international not national obligations. It is a requirement of EU law that FMD diagnosis takes place in a designated national reference laboratory. The Institute for Animal Health at Pirbright is the national reference laboratory for FMD and is also one of 4 OIE reference laboratories for FMD as well as the Food and Agriculture Organisation World Reference Laboratory. The Government accepts the need to support national reference laboratories so they can fully meet all their obligations including, where this is necessary, their OIE reference laboratory function.

RECOMMENDATION	RESPONSE
RS R7.2 Defra should ensure that sufficiently specific and sensitive pen-side antigen detection ELISAs are developed for FMD and other major diseases, are validated as quickly as possible, and are available on a large scale for use in the field, and that a similar ELISA is developed especially for detecting antibodies in sheep. (p84)	Accept in principle. As far as Defra is aware there is no validated field FMD pen-side test currently available. A pen-side test that was under development was not widely used during the 2001 UK outbreak. It is hoped that with further research a dependable FMD test of this type will become attainable. Defra is currently considering funding proposals for research into the application of newer technologies for the diagnosis of FMD and other vesicular diseases. This would include both ELISA and RT-PCR machine based tests. The former is expected to take at least a year before the field-testing can start. The requirement is to develop ELISA tests that are effective for disease detection in all susceptible species, and not just in sheep.
RS R7.3 Defra should explore the potential for portable RT-PCR machines for use in the field or at regional laboratories. (p84)	Accept in principle. See Royal Society recommendation 7.2
RS R7.4 Defra should develop advanced telecommunications between the field and central control. (p84)	Accept. Developments in communications technology will have a continuing impact on ease of communications and the capture and flow of information. During 2002 the State Veterinary Service has carried out a mobile working pilot. This has involved providing laptops, printers, mobile phones, personal digital assistants and in a few cases, digital cameras to veterinary and technical staff in three Animal Health Divisional Offices.
RS R7.5 Defra should consider the benefits of bringing responsibility for all list A diseases under a single organisation. (p84)	Further consideration. The practicality of responding to this recommendation will depend on the outcome of the response to recommendations 10.2 and 10.3.
RS R8.1 The Government should take the lead in developing an international research programme aimed at an improved vaccine that would permit routine and global vaccination of livestock against FMD and other List A diseases. (p105)	Accept in principle. The Government agrees that an improved vaccine that would permit routine and global vaccination of livestock against all strains of FMD is a desirable long-term goal. This is an issue of international rather than national scope and would be most effectively led by an international organisation such as the Food and Agriculture Organisation or possibly as an EU initiative. This issue will be raised in discussions on future research with our EU partners.

RECOMMENDATION	RESPONSE
RS R8.2 Emergency vaccination should be seen as a major tool of first resort, along with culling of infected premises and known dangerous contacts, for controlling FMD outbreaks. This policy should be vaccinate-to-live, which necessitates acceptance that meat and meat products from vaccinated animals enter the food chain normally. (p105)	<u>Accept.</u> See response to Royal Society Key Finding 7.
RS R8.3 In determining the arrangements for deploying emergency vaccination, Defra should: • take account of the urgent need to achieve validation for field use of the tests that discriminate infected from vaccinated animals; • develop emergency vaccination strategies that integrate theoretical and empirical epidemiology and the logistics of delivery of vaccine cover; • establish an exit strategy that takes account of the need for on-going surveillance, safeguards for those involved and agreement that products from vaccinated animals can enter the normal human food chain; (p105)	<u>Accept.</u> The Government is committed to tackling these issues, in consultation with all interested parties, so that it is in a position to trigger an emergency vaccination campaign should the need arise.
RS R8.4 Defra should explore with the EU and OIE what improvements to vaccines and surveillance tests are required to allow disease free status to be based entirely on surveillance results without the requirement for a minimum waiting period. (p105)	<u>Not accepted.</u> Given the UK's interests as an importing country as well as an exporting country the Government believes that there is a need for a minimum waiting period to ensure FMD virus has been eradicated before a country's "FMD free without vaccination" status is restored and trade can be resumed on that basis. The Government therefore does not agree that a minimum waiting period following an outbreak should be entirely abolished.

RECOMMENDATION	RESPONSE
RS R9.1 The main objective in dealing with an outbreak must be to ensure that it does not develop into an epidemic. This requires the following basic measures: i. on suspicion of an outbreak, immediate imposition of strict local movement restrictions and biosecurity measures including culling the animal with clinical signs; ii. on confirmation by an OIE Reference laboratory of an outbreak: ● mobilisation of the full emergency arrangements including all the additional logistic resources and the interdepartmental co-ordination and scientific advisory structure; ● imposition of a total country-wide ban on animal movement with unambiguous and widely publicised advice on the fate of any animals in transit; ● rapid culling of all infected premises; ● identification and rapid culling of all premises where there is a high risk of the disease where these measures are insufficient to guarantee that the outbreak will be contained, we recommend in addition the early deployment of emergency vaccination. (p125)	<u>Accept.</u> The Government has reflected these recommendations in the FMD Contingency Plan. Emergency vaccination should now be considered as part of the control strategy from the start of any outbreak of FMD. Other options, such as additional culling, may be needed depending on the circumstances. Operational plans to vaccinate are being reviewed and developed and a range of scenarios will be used to inform this planning process. The Government's acceptance, in its FMD Contingency Plan and its response to the inquiries, of the recommendation by the Royal Society in favour of an immediate total countrywide ban on animal movements has made the National Audit Office recommendation 10.1 for further research into the imposition of such a ban nugatory. In terms of restrictions on animal movements at other times, both inquiries have made recommendations for a fully considered approach to animal movements. (See Lessons Learned recommendation 61 and Royal Society recommendation 5.3).
RS R9.2 As a matter of urgency, Defra should draw up arrangements for a process for the prior registration for vaccination of zoos and rare breed collections. (p125)	<u>Accept.</u> The Government will discuss implementation of this recommendation with interested parties. The groups of animals will need to be clearly defined in advance. It will also seek EU and international agreement to ensure that this approach would not affect a country's FMD status or the ability to move zoo animals across borders.
RS R9.3 Defra should review its arrangements for other diseases, and in particular the developments required to enable emergency vaccination. (p125)	<u>Accept.</u> Defra is developing a modular disease contingency plan which will include modules relating to emergency vaccination procedures and the control of a range of exotic diseases.

RECOMMENDATION	RESPONSE
RS R9.4 The detailed strategies for controlling outbreaks of livestock diseases should be included in the published contingency plan, which should consist of an umbrella plan for matters that are common to all diseases, with specific modules for each disease. These plans should be rehearsed in an annual "fire drill" that must be realistic and involve Defra and all other relevant bodies including MoD. (p125)	<u>Accept.</u> Work is in hand on a modular approach in the contingency plans, with core modules for structural and operational matters and specific modules for different diseases. Operational exercises both nationally and locally are planned, involving the parties that would be involved in an outbreak.
RS R10.1 The Government should undertake a thorough overhaul of research into animal disease, and in particular develop a national strategy for research in animal disease and surveillance. (p136)	<u>Accept in principle.</u> Co-ordination already exists between research funders for animal health. Defra, BBSRC and Devolved Administrations, as well as private funders, attend each other's reviews of research and develop their research strategies in full knowledge of each other's requirements and current research.

Co-ordination is strongest in the area of Transmissible Spongiform Encephalopathies research where co-ordination with other funders' programmes is achieved through two committees who also arrange workshops so that the funding organisations can monitor the progress of the research and discuss the implications of emerging results. Regular reviews of this kind allow new areas of work and gaps in the programme to be identified.

The Government agrees that co-ordination of research could be strengthened further and is committed to preparing a national Animal Health and Welfare Strategy. During this process Defra will engage with the widest possible interests in its preparation including research institutes, agencies, academics, public and private funders and industry. A significant outcome will be the identification of research requirements for both surveillance and animal disease. Equally research findings will feed back into the Strategy.

An important element of the new Animal Health and Welfare Strategy is the development of a strategy for enhancing veterinary surveillance in the United Kingdom. One of the strategic goals so far identified in an early draft of the strategy is the development of a transparent and open process for prioritising surveillance activities. A key component of this is the

RECOMMENDATION	RESPONSE

collation of information relating to diseases or conditions for which surveillance is to be maintained into "profiles". Relevant information includes epidemiological information about the disease and the availability of suitable diagnostic tests. Collation of such information will facilitate the identification of important gaps in our knowledge, and enable the research work needed to fill these gaps to be identified and prioritised.

This recommendation will provide the focus for taking forward the National Audit Office recommendation 10 for research to be undertaken into the effectiveness and efficiency of measures taken to eradicate FMD and their appropriateness to local circumstances.

RS R10.2 The Government should draw together the current research funding in infectious diseases of animals (both endemic and exotic) within England into a single joint arrangement, the funds being made available to implement the National Strategy; (p136)

Further consideration. Defra accepts the need to strengthen co-ordination and delivery of the research strategy. An Interdepartmental group has met and criteria against which suitable models (both physical and virtual) can be judged and various models have been discussed. These include: similar models to that used for Transmissible Spongiform Encephalopathies research; a single Government organisation managing all funds for animal disease (for instance either the Biotechnology and Biological Sciences Research Council or Defra); or an independent organisation allocated all Government funds and responsible for delivering research requirements. The Government sees value in a model that accesses independent advice and can take a strategic view across this research area. Animal disease research requires expensive facilities and availability of these facilities and expertise should match UK research requirements.

Discussions on the most suitable model are continuing between the funding bodies. This work will be pursued in parallel to the Animal Health and Welfare Strategy and it is planned to reach agreement on a suitable model at the same time that the strategy is produced.

RS R10.3 The Government should create a virtual National Centre for Animal Disease Research and Surveillance, the Board of which would be responsible for delivering the National Strategy; (p136)

Further consideration. See recommendation 10.2 and Key finding 10.

RECOMMENDATION	RESPONSE
RS R10.4 The Government should increase investment in animal disease research and development by the order of £250M over the next 10 years. (p136)	<u>Further consideration.</u> The Government accepts the need for new investment in animal disease research. This is an EU issue and at least part of the programme should be funded at EU level and not necessarily be funded by Defra or the Biotechnology and Biological Sciences Research Council. It is essential that the research needs are identified such that we can agree priorities and funding implications. Work is well in hand to do this as part of the Animal Health and Welfare Strategy.
RS R10.5 Defra should take rapid action to investigate and improve: • the continuous professional development of farmers and stock keepers; • postgraduate training in livestock health and welfare; • the attractiveness of careers within the State Veterinary Service • the training of TVIs and LVIs by Defra, with the RCVS, the BVA and its species divisions, investigating the feasibility of the BCVA proposals. (p138)	<u>Accept in part.</u> Defra is developing a programme to take forward the commitment announced on 26 March to review the effectiveness of training and education for farmers and other land managers. See also Lessons Learned recommendations 3 and 68.

ANNEX II:
RESEARCH INTO ANIMAL HEALTH DISEASES: FUNDING

Defra

1.   Defra's investment in Research and Development on all farm animal diseases and their welfare has risen over the past 10 years from £20.8m to £37.6m in 2001/2. The Department is committed to spend £38.4m in 2003/4. Animal health spending now occupies over 36% of the former MAFF share of the total research budget compared to 19.7% 10 years ago. Exotic animal disease research will receive funding of £4.3m in 2002/3. There has been a process of successive reprioritisation of Defra's annual spend on research into individual farm animal diseases and welfare programmes in response to emerging demands of policy and statutory duties, as well as the need to provide foresight in identifying potential risks for the future.

2.   While the former MAFF total budget for all Research and Development has been under pressure, this has not prevented a range of new and important research investments at the expense of other parts of the agriculture programme. For example, research on Transmissible Spongiform Encephalopathies (TSEs) has risen from about £5.6m in 1995 to its current planned level of over £18m.

3.   The current Defra animal disease research programme, project by project, is set out on the Defra website (http://www.defra.gov.uk/animalh/diseases). In addition the Department devotes more than £50m a year to surveillance, monitoring, surveys and advice on animal diseases which also underpin its work.

4.   All the major funders maintain websites which include details of their research programmes. Defra is also placing final reports on the website and is encouraging researchers to publish their results in peer-reviewed journals. Consultations also take place on research strategies (such as the Biotechnology and Biological Sciences Research Council (BBSRC) Draft Strategic Plan which is now subject to public consultation). Defra will be consulting on its Science and Innovation Strategy next Spring.

Infrastructure

5.   Over £71m has been spent at the Veterinary Laboratories Agency (VLA), most on TSE related accommodation, since the announcement of new-variant Creutzfeldt-Jakob Disease (CJD) in 1996. This accommodation comprises laboratories, associated support accommodation and animal containment facilities both at VLA Weybridge and at various other sites within GB. Some £2m of this work is currently still in hand. In addition between now and early 2005 VLA is undertaking the first phase of the planned redevelopment of its main laboratory site and adjoining farms. Total costs of this first phase will be approximately £63m of which some £20m relates to the provision of a new serology testing laboratory building for large-scale blood testing. This facility would be used in future for testing in the event of large-scale outbreaks of notifiable diseases, e.g. FMD, and will be capable of handling 100,000-120,000 FMD blood samples per week. An extra £6m on top of the original £14m estimated cost was required to construct this laboratory to the appropriate containment standards specifically required for FMD testing.

BBSRC

6.   The current spend on animal disease research by BBSRC is some £25m per annum of which £4.7m is committed to research on exotic diseases. This divides between the funding of the work of, primarily, the Institute for Animal Health and the support provided by the Council funds through research teams and post-graduate research grants at Universities and the veterinary schools. The BBSRC has identified the importance of animal diseases as one of its key themes for strategic investment in its draft Strategic Plan now subject to public consultation (reference: Consultation on Vision and Strategic Plan, http://www.bbsrc.ac.uk/consultation/Welcome.html).

7.   BBSRC will make allocations from its Spending Review settlement later this year in the light of the report and the infrastructure being set up by Defra, the Higher Education Funding Council for England and the Wellcome Trust. BBSRC has identified research into infectious disease in animals as very high priority, particularly research in the fundamental biology of the interactions of a range of infectious organisms with their hosts (viral, bacterial and eukaryotic pathogens) and especially viral persistence; into epidemiology of infectious animal diseases; diagnostics; and into the development of new vaccines. In addition, the recent review of the future of the Institute for Animal Health at Pirbright by Professor Keith Gull has highlighted the need for substantial investment in infrastructure. The current portfolio of animal disease research projects supported by BBSRC can be viewed at http://dataserv.bbsrc.ac.uk/Welcome.html.

Department for International Development (DfID)

8.   DfID funds an Animal Health Research programme to improve the management of livestock disease affecting the livelihoods of poor people in eastern and southern Africa and India. The programme uses the services of UK institutes working closely with developing country partners.

Wellcome trust

9.   The Wellcome Trust has devoted some £7.8m annually to veterinary research over the past 5 years. This covers postgraduate and doctoral awards; fellowships; project/programme grants and the funding of centres in specific disciplines. The Trust supports research on animal diseases on an international level too.

Scottish Executive

10.   The total spending committed to animal health issues by the Scottish Executive Environment and Rural Affairs Department (SEERAD) during 2002/03 is £5.4m, the majority of which is in the form of core funding for the Moredun Research Institute and the Scottish Agricultural College. This funding is devoted primarily to endemic livestock diseases though it provides a platform for the institutes to win contracts from other funders including work on exotic pathogens. Both of these institutes form part of a close network of UK animal health research institutes with complementary remits and skills. And both maintain close links with the Glasgow and Edinburgh University Veterinary Schools through joint appointments and research projects. Indeed SEERAD has jointly funded with the Scottish Higher Education Funding Council a new initiative at the Moredun and the University of Edinburgh to boost veterinary research. SEERAD's funding is guided by its Strategy for Agricultural, Biological and Related Research 1999/2003, under which it aims to fund high quality, effective research, in collaboration with other funders, and relevant to end users.

11.   To this end SEERAD is committed to funding, often with Defra and BBSRC, animal health research that covers a spectrum from strategic through to applied work, in such a manner as to optimise the uptake and application of the research results wherever possible. SEERAD strongly supports the coordination of major funders of animal health research in the UK. It has concordats with BBSRC and Defra and was a member of the Agriculture, Fisheries and Food Research Funders Group. Through these connections SEERAD ensures that the research which it funds at Moredun and at the Scottish Agricultural College is complementary to that funded by the other major funders, and forms an important part of the UK research base in animal diseases.

Northern Ireland

12.   Total expenditure on the Northern Ireland Department of Agriculture and Rural Development's Animal Health and Welfare Research Programme was £807K in the year 2001-2002. Details of the current programme are set out in the relevant pages of the Department's website http://www.dardni.gov.uk/frames/sci11.htm. The mechanisms of prioritisation and commissioning of agriculture and food research in Northern Ireland are currently under review.

ANNEX III:
OPERATIONAL ASPECTS OF EMERGENCY VACCINATION

1.   Contingency plans for emergency vaccination against FMD (including supplies of vaccine, vaccination equipment, staff resources and field instructions) are now being reviewed and extended so that emergency vaccination can be used as part of the overall control strategy.

2.   This process of contingency planning for vaccination will be based upon a range of scenarios and plans and will be reviewed and up-dated on a regular basis. They will be tested on the ground by way of practical emergency exercises involving key stakeholders.

3.   An important logistical issue in relation to vaccination is that of animal identification of vaccinated livestock. Under current EU legislation, restrictions would have to be imposed on all movements of susceptible livestock within and out of a vaccination zone and so identification of vaccinated stock is essential. Identification and tracing of individual cattle is possible with the cattle passport system but there is no equivalent existing system in place for sheep and pigs. Vaccination of sheep or pigs, therefore, would require application of reliable methods of identification, and measures to be put in place to track the subsequent movements of such animals.

4.   To enable emergency vaccination to be introduced rapidly, the SVS's capability will be enhanced by means of a commercially let contract. This contract will be designed to provide an appropriate level of resource and expertise to support the SVS and enable emergency vaccination to be used where appropriate. This contract will be let by way of competitive tender.

5.   The Royal Society report also points to the relevance of emergency vaccination in the conservation of animal biodiversity. It acknowledges that research is needed into the efficacy of vaccines in non-domesticated ruminants and other species and the application of diagnostic tests in such species. The Government accepts the recommendation that Defra should draw up arrangements for the prior registration of zoo collections and rare breeds for possible emergency vaccination against FMD. The groups of animals concerned will need to be clearly defined in advance. The UK will seek EU and OIE agreement that the vaccination of zoo animals will not affect a country's FMD status.

6.   The Government is currently reviewing vaccine supplies both at a national and international level. The UK is a member of the International Vaccine Bank, the European Union's Vaccine Bank, and owns a national stock of vaccine. The Government agrees with the Royal Society that for a vaccination-to-live policy it will be essential to have full Marketing Authorisations for the relevant vaccines. The Government is working towards fulfilling this for the main strains of the FMD virus. The Government will also be seeking assurances from the EU that the antigens held in its bank meet our requirements.

Printed in the UK for The Stationery Office Limited
on behalf of the Controller of Her Majesty's Stationery Office
11/02   C118026
Printed on recycled paper containing 75% post consumer waste and 25% ECF